Published by Aeon Press 2006



ISBN 0 9534784 6 8

Printed and bound in Ireland by:
Colour Books Ltd.
105 Baldoyle Industrial Estate
Dublin 13.

Aeon Press
8 Bachelor's Walk
Dublin 1
Ireland.
email: sales@yellowbrickroad.ie
URL: www.yellowbrickroad.ie

Illustrations: Denise O'Moore
Photography: John Smails

# Contents


| | |
|---|---|
| Introduction | Page 6 |
| Equipment | Page 7 |
| Threading Materials | Page 11 |
| Findings | Page 15 |
| Beads | Page 19 |
| Project 1: Hair Clip | Page 20 |
| Project 2: Standard Drop Earring | Page 21 |
| Project 3: Swing Earrings | Page 22 |
| Project 4: Leather Thong Necklace | Page 23 |
| Project 5: Suede Lace Necklace | Page 25 |
| Project 6: Cotton Thong Necklace | Page 27 |
| Project 7: Floating Bead Necklace | Page 29 |
| Project 8: Floating Earrings | Page 31 |
| Project 9: Threaded Necklace | Page 33 |
| Project 10: Stud Earrings | Page 37 |
| Project 11: Link Bracelet | Page 38 |
| Project 12: Necklace Without Findings | Page 39 |
| Project 13: Fairies and Angels | Page 42 |
| Project 14: Memory Wire Bracelet | Page 43 |
| Project 15: Wine Identity Ring | Page 45 |
| Project 16: Memory Wire Choker | Page 46 |
| Project 17: Wired Necklace | Page 48 |
| Project 18: Organza Necklace | Page 52 |

# INTRODUCTION

Making your own jewellery can be a daunting task when you are unfamiliar with the vast array of beads and components. Where to start? What threading materials are best for the beads you have chosen? What tools to use? How to finish off your jewellery so that it looks professional?

Creating jewellery is a rewarding pastime and a profitable business. Once you have mastered a few basic techniques and added your imagination, you can create a style of your own. Your jewellery can be expensive or inexpensive, contemporary or dated, plain or intricate, the choice will be yours. Experiment with the materials, vary the techniques, mix and blend the components, and dip into the wealth of beads and findings now available.

Reading carefully through the instructions of each project in this book before starting will help you to understand what is involved. Starting a project at the beginning of this book and making your way through it will gradually increase your skills. The last projects are more intricate than the first.

I have mixed metric and imperial measurements as jewellery is often referred to in inches - a 16" necklace for example. However metric measurements are easier to write and describe and most beads are now measured in millimetres.

There are no rules, only guidelines. What matters most, is that what you have made pleases you or the person you are giving it to. Above all else, enjoy creating.

# Equipment

One of the advantages to jewellery-making as a profession or hobby is that there is very little initial outlay. As your interest develops you can invest in more specialised tools if you need to. To get started the following list of tools and equipment will be adequate. Most, but not all, are used in this book. The right tools for the job certainly make your work easier, tidier and more efficient.

When using the tools at first you may feel all fingers and thumbs. With practice you will become more nimble-fingered and will find yourself easily manipulating the materials with a tool in each hand.

**1. Round Nose Pliers**
Essential for making well rounded loops and for bending wire smoothly.

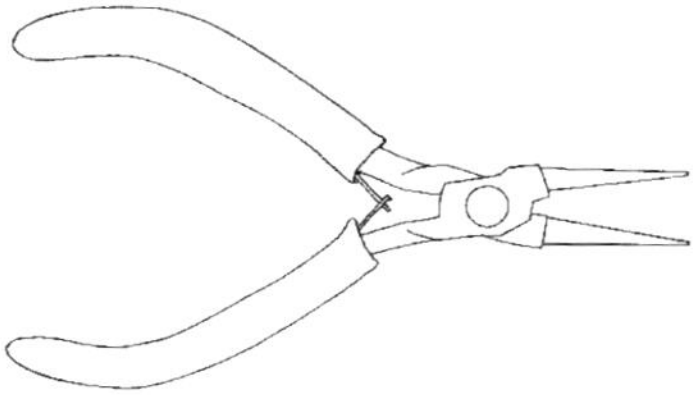

**2. Chain Nose Pliers**
Used for gripping wire and jump rings etc. and general use.

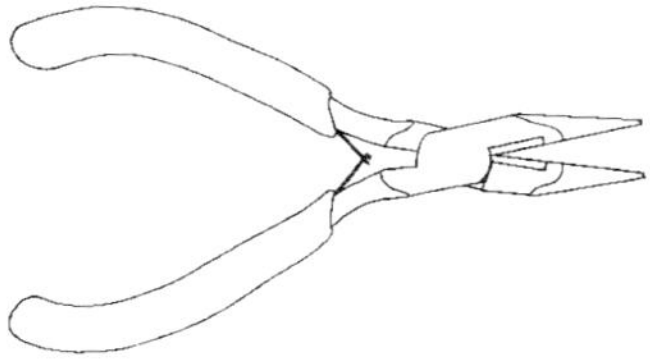

**3. Bent Nose Pliers**
A handy tool used in much the same way as the chain nose pliers except this tool curves and can reach difficult places more easily.

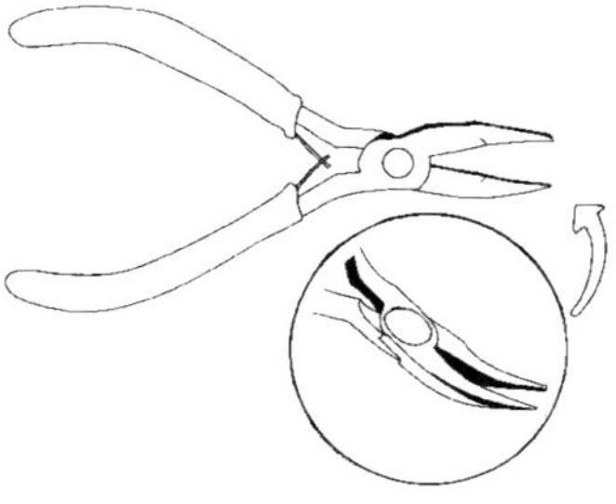

**4. Side Cutters**
For cutting headpins and other wires. These pliers will give a pointed cut.

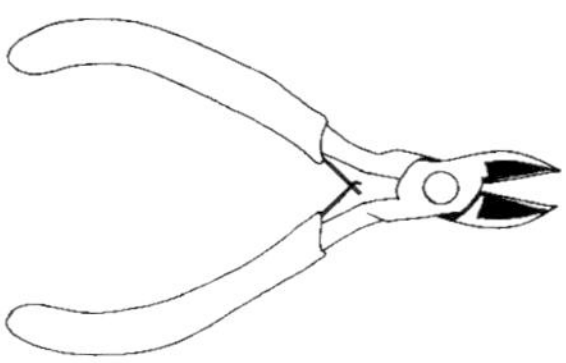

### 5. Crimping Tool

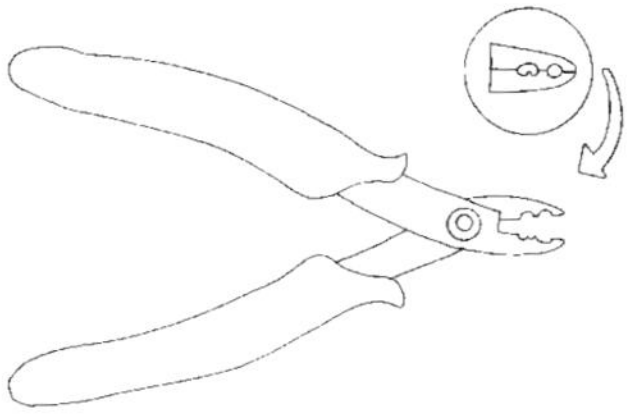

The crimping tools shapes then re-forms a crimp (see findings on page 12) into a sphere. There are two types available at present, one being a micro-crimper making the crimp smaller than the regular crimper.

### 6. Flush Cutters

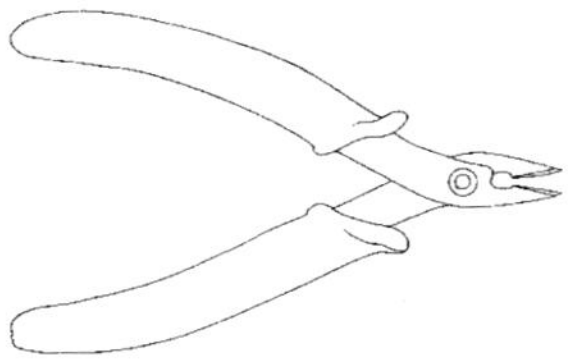

Also used for cutting wires etc. except these pliers will leave a straight edged cut.

### 7. Awl

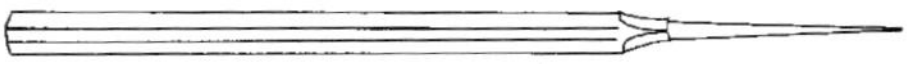

Used for drawing knots close together, for loosening knots and for removing blockages from the centre of beads.

### 8. Beading Needles

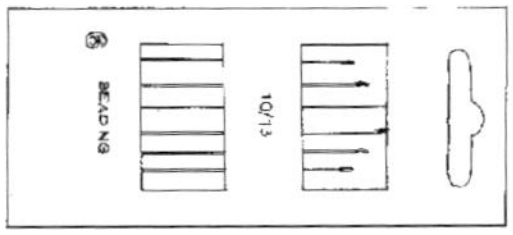


These are especially fine needles that are compatible with beading threads, readily available in packages of 6 needles, marked 10/13. These figures refer to the size of needles, size 10 being larger and easier to thread than size 13. **Sharps** are short and fine and are used for off-loom work.There are also much longer beading needles available which are used for loom work.

**Big Eye** needles are a wonderful invention, especially for those who have trouble threading needles. They are available in two sizes : 2.25" or 4.5" and are quite thick. As a result they are not suitable for fine beadwork. Almost the full length of the needle is an eye. It opens like a bow (as in bow and arrow).When using one of these, bear in mind that the inside of this needle is sharp and the thread you have put inside it should be moved along regularly otherwise the sharpness of the interior of the needle will cut your thread.

## 9. Glues

Hypo tube cement can be used for extra security inside a callotte (see findings on page 16). It is particularly useful in jewellery-making as it has a nozzle the diameter of a pin, allowing precision.

E6000 is a very strong slow drying glue. It is thick and a little messy to work with. However it is worth waiting for as it will stick your project permanently .

Generally speaking the faster the glue dries the quicker it dehydrates resulting in the glue losing its adhesion. Unfortunately there is not one glue that does everything.

## 10. Scissors

A small sharp scissors is essential to obtain a clean cut.

## 11. Bead Design Board

These are available in a variety of lengths and styles. They are very helpful when planning out your latest project. Being able to leave your work on it allows you to resume your project easily. If you need to keep your expenses down try making your own out of jumbo ribbed corduroy, marking out the measurements with an indelible felt pen. For further economy substitute the corduroy with corrugated paper from an art supply shop.

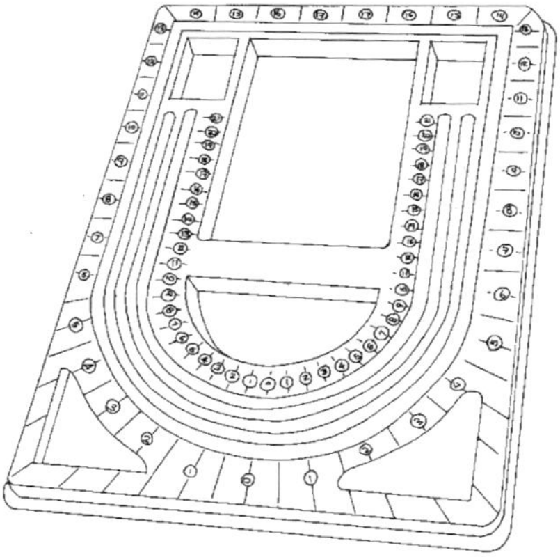

## 12. Ring Mandrel

This word appears to have many interpretations. The one given is jewellery related. In loose terms it means a tubular form with which to hold work. This is a long ( approx 12") tapered tool used for forming the exact size of a ring. The end closest to the handle will yield the largest ring size. The sizes written along the circumference of the mandrel correspond with the ring sizers below.

13. Ring Sizers

These are obtained in a bunch of 29 different ring sizes catering from child size to adult. The idea is that you slip your finger into the ring that is most comfortable for you enabling you to judge the exact size to fit. Used in conjunction with the mandrel above, will provide consistent results.

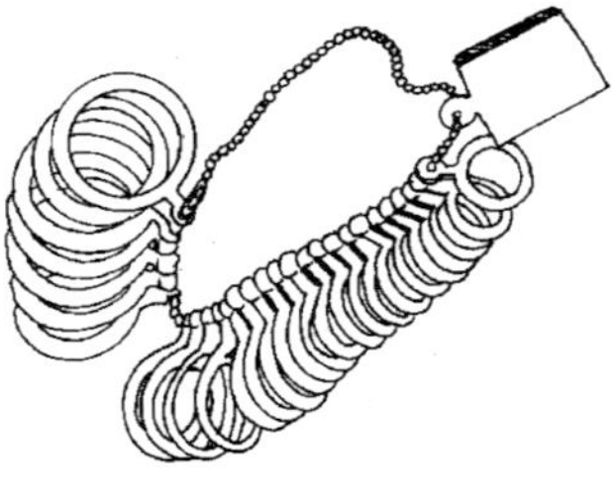

**14. Beading Mat**

An invaluable tool. These mats are fleecy and prevent beads and other small items from meandering every which way off the table. They are available in many colours and the 12"x 10" size is freely available. However, 2 colours are handy to have in your kit: a darkish one to show up against pale materials and a light one to show up against dark materials.

**15. Dual System Measuring Tape**

These are worth tracking down. One side has inches only. The other side has inches running along the bottom half and the metric system running along the top. This allows you to assess the corresponding equivalent of both systems at the same time. It helps take some of the trepidation out of swapping from one system to another.

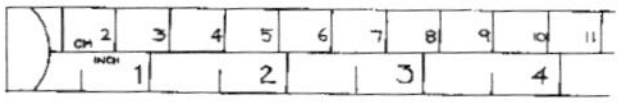

# Threading Materials

It is difficult to keep up with the ever-changing variety of threading materials coming onto the market. Commonly available in a variety of colours and thicknesses are polyester, nylon filament, silk, elastic, cotton thong, leather thong, suede lace, rat-tail, hemp, organza ribbon, wire mesh, nylon coated wires and even PVC. There has been an increase in wirework jewellery, and as a result there is a greater choice in colour and quality of wires. Each material offers a different effect and some materials are suited to different types of beads and consequently different types of findings.

**Silk**

Traditionally used for stringing pearls, it is also used for a wide variety of projects. While it is a wonderfully soft and tactile product available in many colours, silk tends to stretch and easily absorbs dirt.

**Carded Needled Cord**

There is a large range of threads made of both polyamid and silk which come on a card with a needle already integrated into the thread. When the thread is being manufactured the needle is slipped on to the thread and then the thread is twisted, therefore the needle eye is similar in diameter to the thread, or even smaller. But beware, polyamid frays very easily. You need to plan your design accurately as polyamid is only usable via the integrated needle. **See project 9**.

**Polyester**

A strong threading material primarily used in sewing, this will suffice for necklace making purposes only if beading thread is not available.

**Elastic**

Sheering elastic can be useful for bracelets. Clear rubber-like elastic can be found in bead shops in many colours. Children find elastic easy to handle as they can slip an elasticised bracelet over their small hands. It is a fun, quick and an easy-to-use product but anything that stretches will eventually weaken and break.

**Thonging**

This is the word used to describe a leather or cotton strand. It is commonly available in thicknesses of .5mm to 2.0mm and in a wide variety of colours, though everyone uses black. It is used for threading with beads which have a hole matching the diameter of the thonging. It is long lasting and is widely used for pendants and projects using large holed beads. **See projects 4 and 12**.

**Suede Lace**

This is flattened strips of suede and usually costs more than leather thong. It is available in a wide choice of colours. Imitation suede is an equally versatile substitute and is cheaper. **See project 5**.

**Rat-tail**

Satin-like thonging that comes in 2mm diameter thickness. When it comes in 1mm thickness it is called mouse tail. It is soft and silky and has a wide range of colours.

**Nylon Coated Wire**

Tigertail is a commonly accepted generic word for plastic coated wire produced by a number of cable manufacturing companies. It consists of several strands of wire coated in plastic. It varies from 7 strands of coated wire up to 49 strands per coated wire. The more strands there are, the more supple the wire. There are many brand names of this product and many quality differences.

It is one of the strongest materials around and is excellent for use with gemstone beads which are very often heavy and rough on the inside.

Conversely it is very effective when used to make a floating necklace using lightweight beads. **See project 7**

The advantages are many, the disadvantages only few. Because it is primarily a wire, it tends to knot poorly and has a tendency to kink, so some caution is required when handling it. As a rule of thumb, the more strands used to form the product, the more supple and knottable it is; the more supple the product, the higher the price. To overcome the knotting problem use crimps to secure beads and findings.

This can be a difficult material to cut. Use a flush cutters or failing that a sharp pair of nail clippers can do the trick. Experiment. **See project 8**.

**Nymo**

This is a brand name for thread that was originally produced for the upholstery industry. It has been welcomed by bead workers as it is a strong nylon thread with an extensive size and colour range. Size A is the finest and size G is the thickest. Sizes B and D are most commonly used.

Though this thread is fine and surprisingly strong, it is not intended for use with heavy beads.

**Wire**

This is available in a wonderful array of colour, gauge (thickness) and quality, each one giving the designer more scope to create. Generally speaking, the very fine wire, 34 gauge, has a smaller colour range than the more widely used sizes of 28, 26, and 24 gauge for example. The higher the number, the finer the wire. Wire is also measured in millimetres (in Europe), 0.4mm, 0.6mm, 0.8mm and 1.0mm being the most popular sizes; the latter is useful for making your own fasteners. Wire is used effectively in project 17.

**Memory Wire**

This is a pre-formed wire which stays in a permanent coil. It is aptly named as it always returns to its original shape and is extremely tough. When cutting this wire I recommend that you use that hard pair of pliers in the toolshed because cutting memory wire will destroy the neat precision pliers you bought for jewellery making. If you find that this is the medium for you and create a lot of memory wire jewellery, you could splash out and buy a tool specifically designed for cutting this wire. It does the trick like no other, though it is not cheap.

Memory wire is currently available in silver and gold colours in both matt and shiny finshes. There are at least four sizes: ring, bracelet ( small and large ) and choker.

The ring size can also be used as a toe ring or to make delightful wine glass identity rings. **See project 15**. All types can be used to make jewellery in a single coil or multiple coils. Wrap around your finger, wrist or neck once or several times. It is great for an instant item of jewellery as there are no fasteners or additional findings required. **See projects 14 and 16**.

**Nylon Monofilament**

This is fishing line. The only constructive comment to make on this material is that it is useful for temporary stringing. Because it is photo degradable, it disintegrates. It cracks, melts, ages, kinks, and stretches. Once damage of this magnitude occurs it is just a matter of time before your jewellery ends up on the floor. There are many much better alternatives.

**Braided Nylon**

There are a number of companies producing a plaited multi-stranded nylon cord. It is currently available in a restricted colour range and a few diameters. They are often referred to as braided bead thread and are commonly available in size D (.008 of an inch / 0.2 mm) and size B (.006 of an inch / .15 mm). When you read ‘multi stranded’ you imagine a thick material but actually the fine edition of these threads mentioned above can slip through the eye of a beading needle. It is strong, flexible, practically non-stretch and almost invisible. A far better solution than monofilament.

**Wire Mesh Ribbon**

This is a unique material made of very finely knitted wire which is produced in a seamless tube which gets flattened when rolled on the cone it is sold from. It is

produced in 2 diameters though it is most commonly available in the 5mm width. It has a wonderful colour range and is a remarkably versatile material. As it is tubular wire it is possible to pull the wire in opposing directions resulting in a ruffled effect. Bear in mind that if you buy a metre of mesh and then ruffle the sides the length will decrease as it shrinks width wise.
As it is a tube it is possible to fill the tube with beads with either one large bead or a selection of small ones. This material will be explored in book 2.

**Organza Ribbon**
This is a delightful light ribbon made from organza. It has a wide colour range and is available in diameters from 4mm to 10mm. Threading beads or a light pendant onto the ribbon looks pretty and feminine. **See project 18.**

**Chain**
There are many styles and finishes available in chain. It can be used to great effect in jewellery making. Open the links of chain and add beads in between. **See projects 3 and 17.**

**Hemp**
Is the fibre from the hemp plant originating in India. It is used primarily in 1mm and 2mm thickness for jewellery making purposes. It is most commonly available in a a kind of oatmeal colour. Hemp jewellery is based on macramé knotting.

**Mastex**
Another material originally produced for the upholstery trade, it can also be used as a stringing material for making jewellery. It is a popular fibre for crochet to which beads can be added. It is made of two strands of twisted nylon, has a muted colour range, is supple and strong but has only one thickness. It can fray a little. When inserting mastex into a bead twist it clockwise into the bead, this helps to prevent unravelling. Keep the tip of this fibre neatly cut.

# Findings

Findings is the collective name for all the small metal components used in jewellery making. They are available in a varied range of finishes. Most are available in gold and silver plate, surgical steel, niobium, sterling silver, rolled gold and gold. In recent years most plated findings are nickel safe. This means that there is only trace amounts of nickel in the base metals. A lot of people are highly allergic to nickel. Some base metals have a colour range such as black, bronze or copper. Niobium can have a vivid colour range of fuchsia, purple, green and other bright colours.

Generally speaking the findings are best kept small and neat as you don't want to attract attention to these functional components. Having said that, sometimes the catches are so attractive that you make them into a feature in their own right, after all if you have short hair or wear your hair up, the back of your neck is on view. Bracelets tend to rotate and invariably roll catch side up.

The findings mentioned in this book are readily available and commonly used for basic jewellery making. There is nothing more informative however than spending some time mooching around your local bead shop for findings that are a bit out of the ordinary. Pretty, neat findings really add the finishing touch giving your jewellery that professional edge. The choices and combinations are endless.

**Bolt Rings:** available in a number of sizes from 5mm up to 10mm and are used in conjunction with a tag to close necklaces, bracelets etc.

**Trigger Catches:** available from 5mm to 12m sizes for jewellery making purposes and are also used in conjunction with a tag.

**Torpedo Screws:** have two parts - one screws into the other. Generally speaking anything that screws together easily, also unscrews easily too.

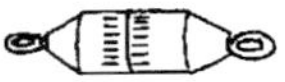

**Barrel Screws:** sturdier than torpedo screws, hence they are a little more reliable.

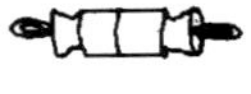

**Fancy Catches:** these come in a very wide choice as the mechanism is the same but the shell can be a multitude of designs. They can be a little difficult to manipulate but are secure.

**Spring Ends:** Strong, tightly coiled wire tubes; they are inserted over leather or cotton thonging allowing other findings to be attached.

**Hook Catch:** these are used primarily with spring ends or fold-over crimps.

**Fold-Over Crimp:** used to secure flat strips of leather or suede lace allowing other findings to be secured.

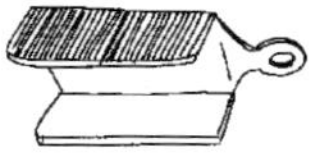

**Clamshell Calottes:** top opening: primarily used to hide unsightly knots and crimps. They are most commonly available in one size. **For an example see project 9**.

**Side Opening Calottes:** these are available in two sizes: standard and large. They have a sealed loop as opposed to the open hook of other calottes. The are useful to have in your findings kit as they can be added after your design is finished. **Used in Project 8 or 11.**

**Toggle Clasp:** a practical way to fasten a bracelet as you can open and close this catch with one hand, eliminating the need to ask anyone for help. They also work very nicely as fasteners for necklaces. They have a wide variety of sizes and designs. **See Project 5 or 12**.

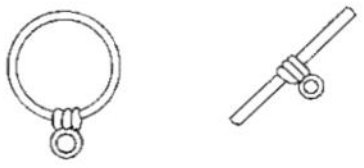

**Crimps:** tiny bead-like metal components that are specially designed to squash. They are often used in conjunction with tiger tail to secure beads and findings. It is not advisable to use them with thread as they are metal the crimps would break it. **See projects 5, 7 or 13.**

**Eye Pins:** these are used to link or extend earrings bracelets etc. There is a small loop at one end called an eye. They are widely used in jewellery making. **See project 11.**

**Head Pins:** the foundation on which most earrings are built. They are an integral part of jewellery making. They have a small head on the tip of each one preventing the beads from falling off. **See project 2.**

**Fish Hooks:** one of the most popular earring findings.

**Kidney Wires:** made of thinner wire than most earring findings, they have the added security of folding back onto a hook. They usually cost less than other earring hooks.

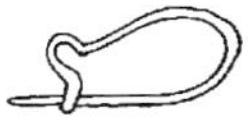

**Euro Hooks:** offer the best of both worlds. They drop like a fish hook, have the security of kidney wire but are made of a sturdier metal. Needless to say, they will cost a little extra. **See matching earrings to project 9.**

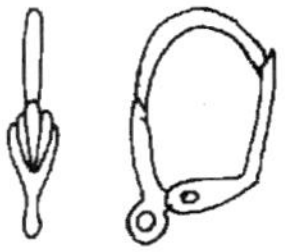

**Ear Studs:** available in a range of styles and sizes, they offer the wearer a shorter earring by sitting against the ear. **See matching earrings to project 5.**

**Flat Pad Studs:** have a number of diameter pads which can be oval or round. A cabochon (a rhinestone or stone that is flat on the back and domed at the front) can be glued on to the pad. **See project 10.**

**Scrolls:** used to secure studs in place at the back of the ear, they are sometimes known as butterflies.

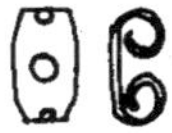

**Ear Screws:** used for non-pierced ears and are screwed into place from the back of the ear. They are seen mostly on old jewellery. Clip-on earrings are another alternative for non-pierced ears.

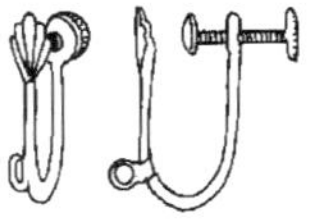

**Bead Cups:** can enhance the plainest of beads giving prominence and focus to the finished piece. Available in a wonderful assortment of styles and sizes, they can also act as a stopper on the end of a head pin when the bead hole is too big and the bead could fall over the headpin.

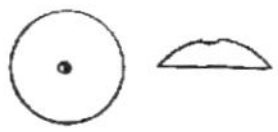

**Tag:** used in conjunction with bolt rings and lobster claws as closure for a necklace or bracelet.

**Hair Clips:** Readily available in 4 different sizes: 40mm, 60mm, 80mm and 100mm. Nickel or silver plate are the most readily available finishes.

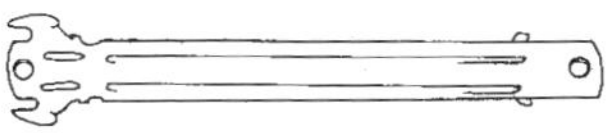

**Metal Beads:** it is surprising what a big difference these tiny beads make to your jewellery. They seem to add finality to a sequence of beads. They are most commonly used in jewellery making in sizes 2.5m, 3mm and 4mm.

**Jump Rings:** these look like insignificant little circles but are in fact a vital part of jewellery making. They are used to link other findings together, often giving movement to your jewellery. They are readily available as small as 3mm up to 9mm and in different thicknesses.

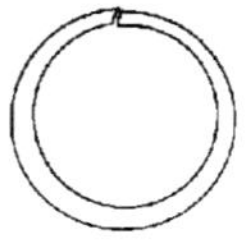

Fig 1

**TIP**

**Opening a jump ring:**

**1.)** Holding the bent nose pliers point upward with your left hand, grip the side of the jump ring (Fig. 2). Please note that the join of the jump ring is central.

**2.)** With the chain nose pliers in your right hand grip the other side of the jump ring (Fig. 2).

**3.)** Turn your wrists in opposite directions, opening the jump ring. Close the jump ring in the same way but in reverse.

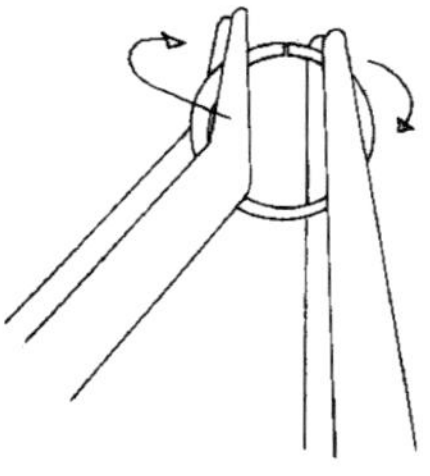

Fig 2

This technique enables you to open and close the jump ring accurately, preventing any gaps appearing between the join. If that gap is not tight any subsequent links will slip through. Your work is only as strong as the weakest link. Pulling the jump ring outwards will result in distortion of the circle.

# BEADS

Beads have been used as adornment since the beginning of time. People have threaded animal claws and bones onto string and worn them as trophies and talismans. In cultures all over the world beads have been worn to demonstrate a person's wealth, marital status, profession, gender, and age.

Today beads are big business. They are more popular now than ever before and are produced in their billions every day. In some countries, like India for example, entire villages still practice the same handmade methods that have been used for centuries. The quality has now vastly improved as have the techniques for bead making. Japanese manufacturers use the latest technology to make the finest quality beads, particularly seed beads and Delicas (similar to seed beads, but cylindrical in shape). The Czech Republic has a long standing tradition for bead making and have a thriving industry today. Austria produce top quality lead crystal beads. Venice is one of the original glass bead producers and are still in the forefront today. Their techniques are highly prized secrets. These and many other countries contribute to a wealth of continually changing choice.

Beads can be and are made from practically anything. You can even make your own out of cloth or paper. Beads come in all sizes. Tiny beads are called seed beads because they look like seeds. They are also known as Love Beads as they were often given as a token of love, particularly during the sixties and seventies. Another word commonly used for seed beads is Rocailles, meaning little rock in French. Anything from these tiny beads up to a large hunk of clay with a hole drilled through it.

Beads are readily available in wood, bone, ceramic, glass, plastic, porcelain, clay, amber, coral, jet, precious and semi precious stone, metals, silver and gold. Only elephants should wear ivory. The world is your oyster or should I say your pearl. There is no end to the variety and choice and no limit to the combinations.

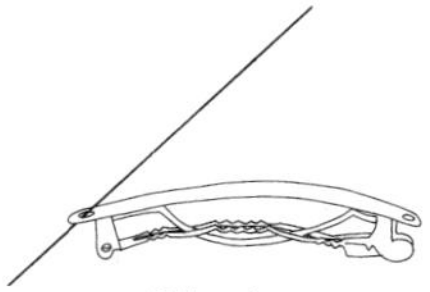

Fig 1

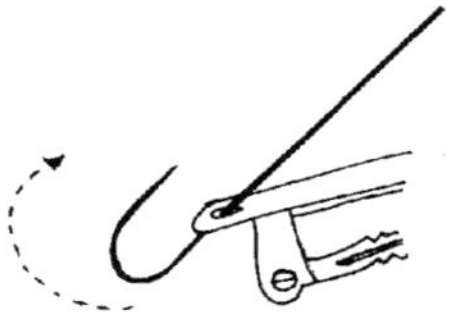

Fig. 2

Fig 3

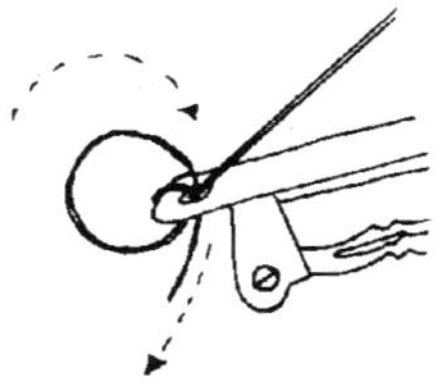

Fig 4

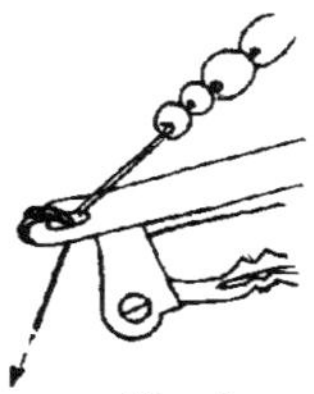

Fig 5

An attractive way to decorate a hair clip is to cover it with beads. These can be quite expensive to buy in the shops.

To make the hairclip pictured you will need the following :

**Materials:**
1 x 80mm hair clip
15mm of 0.6mm wire
4 x 4mm fibre optic beads
4 x 8mm barrel beads
6 x 6mm beaded discs
4 x 2.5mm metal beads
1 x 15mm flower/feature bead
Alternatively, substitute where desired

**Tools:**
Chain Nose Pliers
Cutters

**Method:**

**1.)** Pass approximately 2.5cm of wire through the hole at any end of the clip (Fig.1).

**2.)** Bend the wire back into the hole and pull reasonably taut with the chain nose pliers (Fig. 2 & 3). Be careful not to pull the wire too hard in case it breaks. Repeat this procedure once more (Fig. 4).

**3.)** Cut off any excess wire and flatten any remaining wire against the hair clip to avoid catching in your hair or clothes.

**4.)** Thread the beads on to the wire as shown (Fig. 5) or as desired.

**5.)** Secure the beads by finishing in the same way as you started, following steps 1, 2, 3 & 4.

## Project 2 - Standard Drop Earrings

These earrings are easily made by threading beads onto a headpin which has a small tip on the end to prevent the beads from falling off. If the bead hole is larger than the tip of the headpin try threading on a metal bead, seed bead or cup before adding the main beads.

To make the earrings pictured you will need the following:

**Materials:**
2 x 18mm cloisonné drop beads
2 x 2 inch headpins
2 x fish hooks
6 x seed beads
2 x 6mm bicone beads
4 x 4mm beaded discs
4 x small cups
Alternatively, substitute where desired

**Tools:**
Round Nose Pliers
Cutters

**Method:**
**1.)** Thread the beads on to the headpin in the desired sequence.
**2.)** Leaving a tiny gap after the last bead added on (this gap is the diameter of the narrowest end of the pliers), bend the headpin at a right angle with the round nose pliers (Fig.1).
**3.)** From the bend, measure between 6mm and 9mm of the exposed headpin then cut off any remainder. The longer the remaining length of headpin, the further up the nose of the pliers you will need to go.
**4.)** With the round nose pliers, grip the end of this wire (Fig.2) - the further up the pliers you go the larger the loop. Roll the wire back towards the top of the earring to form a well rounded loop (Fig. 3).
**5.)** Open the loop just formed and attach a fish hook (Fig. 4). Close the loop.
**6.)** Repeat to complete the other earring.

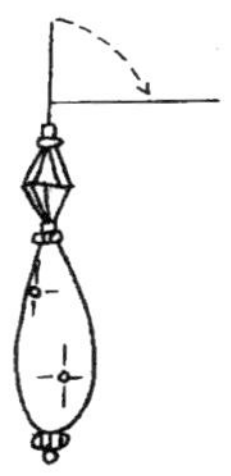
Fig 1

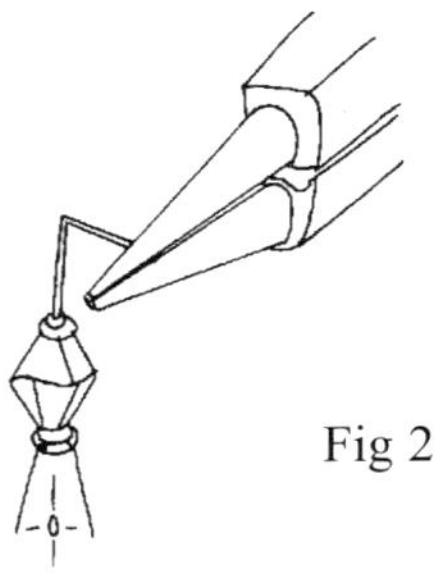
Fig 2

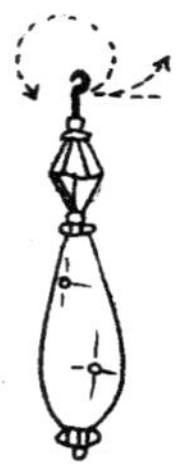
Fig 3

Fig 4

# Project 3 - Swing Earrings

Fig 1

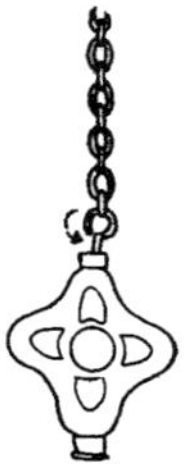

Fig 2

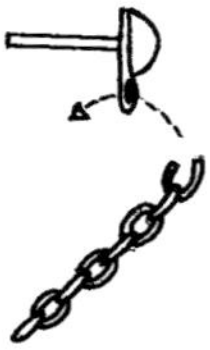

Fig 3

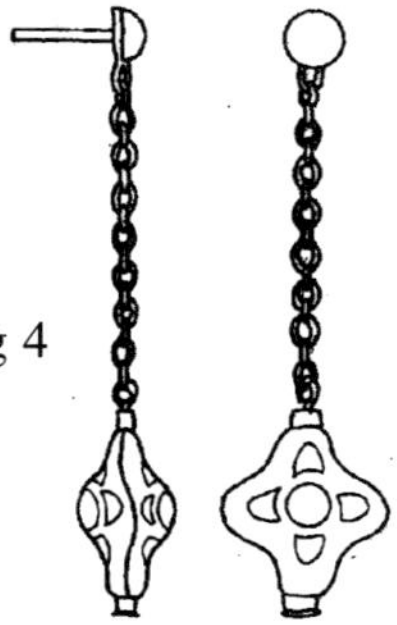

Fig 4

These earrings have movement and can be easily adapted by changing the chain lengths, altering the bead type or adding more beads. When purchasing chain for this project try to get chain with links that are openable. If this type of chain is not available use jump rings to link the chain and beads together.

To make the earrings pictured you will need the following:

**Materials:**
6cm of 2mm link belcher chain - gold plate
2 x 14mm cloisonné diamond shaped beads
4 x 11° seed beads
2 x domed stud earring findings
2 x scrolls
Alternatively, substitute where desired

**Method:**
**1).** Thread the beads on to the head pins as desired. Make a loop at the top of these beads as shown in project 2.
**2.)** Cut the chain into 2 lengths with 16 complete chain links in each length.
**3.)** Open the loop just formed on the headpin and slip the last link of one end of the chain on to this loop (Fig. 1) and close this loop again (Fig. 2).
**4.)** Open the last link at the other end and slip the loop of the stud over this link (Fig 3). Close the link. If your chain does not open, link these two parts together with a jump ring.
**5.)** Fit scroll to the back of the stud.
**6.)** Repeat to complete the other earring.

## Project 4 - Leather Thong Necklace

This project has a pendant with a hole through left to right (horizontally) making bead threading straightforward. If your favourite pendant has a hole going directly through it from front to back, then simply pass the thonging through the hole and tie an overhand knot using both strands directly above the pendant. Proceed as directed below. Alternatively put a large jump ring through the pendant hole and then thread the leather through the jump ring.

To make the necklace pictured you will need the following :

**Materials:** (to make a 17 inch necklace)
1 x 16 ½" length of 2mm leather thong
2 x spring ends
1 x hook catch
1 x pendant
4 x 8mm ceramic beads
8 x 4mm ceramic beads
10 x metalised plastic discs
2 x 8mm spiral beads
2 x 15mm spiral beads
Alternatively, substitute where desired

**Tools:**
Chain Nose Pliers
Cutters

**Method:**
**1.)** Thread beads onto leather as demonstrated in the picture or as desired. If you have difficulty getting the beads onto the thonging, cut the tip of the leather into a point (Fig.1).
**2.)** Allow the beads to fall to the centre of the leather strand. Insert the leather into the spring end. Allow the back of the pliers to rest against the last complete rung of the spring end, the front of the pliers rest on the ½ rung at the front of the spring end. The last rung is only a ½ coil. Depress the ½ coil against the back of the pliers

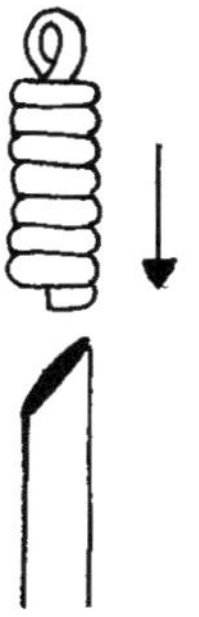
Fig 1

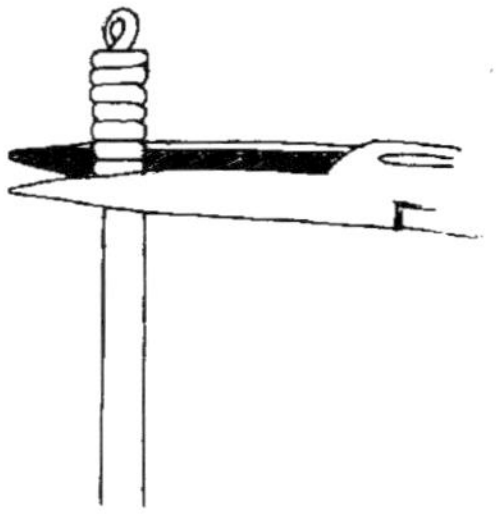
Fig 2

Fig 3

(Fig.2). Repeat for the other side.
**3.)** Clip the hook onto the loop of the spring end on the right hand side (if you are right handed) and pull the hook down so that it squeezes into the eye of the hook (Fig. 3).

**NOTE**

Most fastenings take up between ½ an inch to 1 inch.
Adjust the length of threading material dependant on the wearer's height in order for a pendant to sit in the centre of the collar bone.

## Matching Earrings

**Materials:**
2 x headpins
2 x 8mm dome studs
4 x 3mm metal beads
4 x small plain cups
4 x metalised plastic discs
2 x 4mm ceramic beads
2 x 8mm spiral bead

**Tools:**
Round Nose Pliers
Cutters

**Method:**
**1.)** Thread the beads on to the head pin as depicted in the picture.
**2.)** Follow instructions for standard earrings - **project 2**.

Project 1
Hair Clip

Project 2
Drop Earring

Project 3
Swing Earring
Project 14
Memory Wire
Bracelet

Project 4
Leather Thong
Necklace

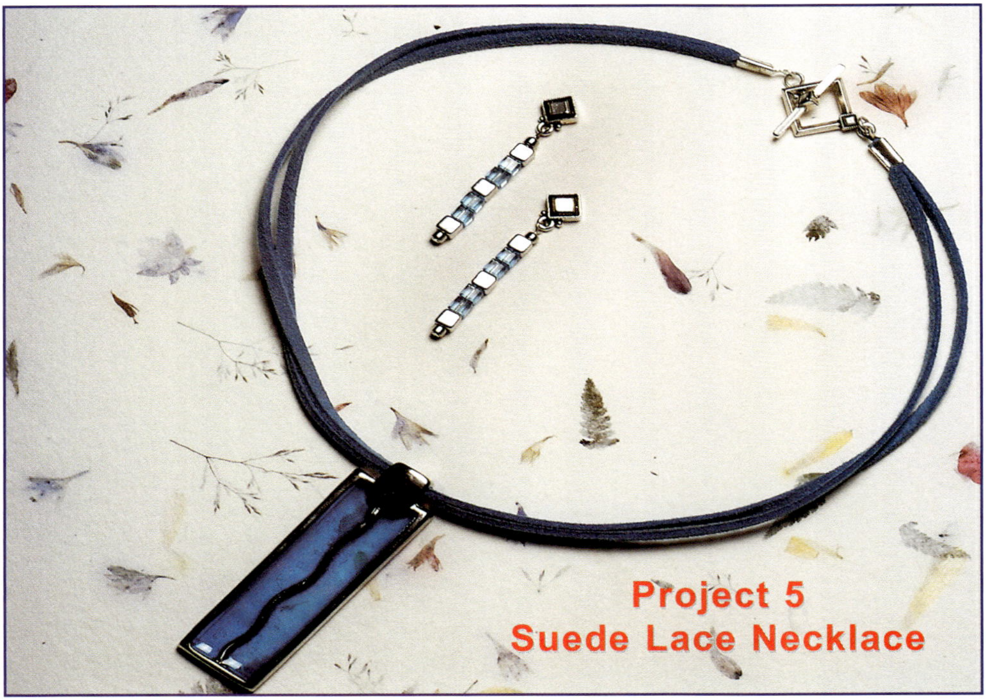
Project 5
Suede Lace Necklace

Project 6
Cotton Thong
Necklace

Project 7
Floating
Necklace
Project 8
Floating Earrings

Project 17
Wired Necklace

Project 11
Link Bracelet

Project 9
Threaded Necklace

**Project 16
Memory Wire
Choker**

**Project 12
Necklace
Without
Findings**

Project 15
Wine Identity Ring

Project 13
Fairies and Angels

Project 10
Stud Earrings

Project 18
Organza Necklace

## Project 5 - Suede Lace Necklace

Imitation suede has been used for this project, the colour range is so enticing.
The plain uncomplicated lines of this piece make for a casual day-to-day necklace.

To make the necklace pictured you will need the following:

**Materials:**
2 x 15 inch lengths of 4mm flat imitation suede lace
2 x 7mm flat fold-over crimp
1 x horizontally drilled pendant
3 x 4mm jump rings
1 x 22mm diamond toggle catch
Alternatively, substitute where desired

**Tools:**
Bent Nose pliers
Cutters

**Method:**
**1.)** Slide the pendant onto both pieces of suede ensuring both ends are of an even length.
**2.)** Trim the suede so that it is even at both ends. Place both ends of one side into a crimp (Fig. 1). Fold the right hand wing of the crimp over both pieces of suede with the bent nose pliers (Fig. 2). Pinch the top and the bottom as well to ensure the crimp has been flattened all the way along.
**3.)** Turn the work around and with the bent nose pliers fold the remaining wing over the previous one (Fig. 3). Pinch the top and bottom as before. Repeat the same for the other side.
**4.)** Open the jump ring as shown on page 18. Slip loop of the fold-over crimp onto the jump ring. As the jump ring is still open, slip another jump ring onto it. Close this jump ring. You will now have two jump rings attached to the fold-over crimp. Open the second jump ring and slip the loop of the T in the toggle onto this jump ring. Close it again (Fig.4). The reason there are two jump rings on this side and only one on the other is because the two jump rings act as a mini chain giving more freedom for the 'T'

Fig 1
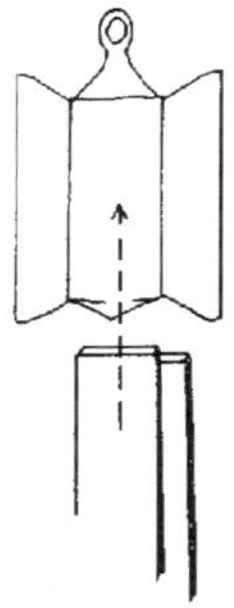

Fig 2
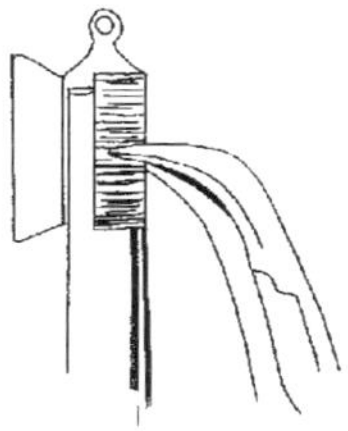

Fig 3
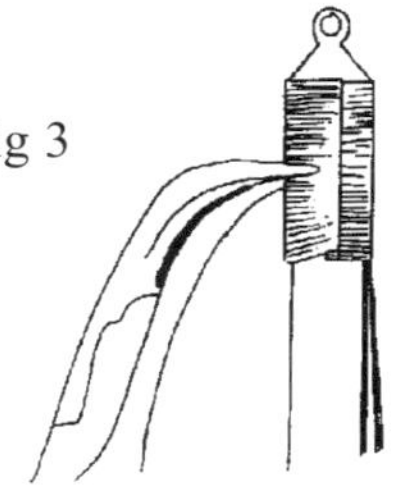

Fig 4

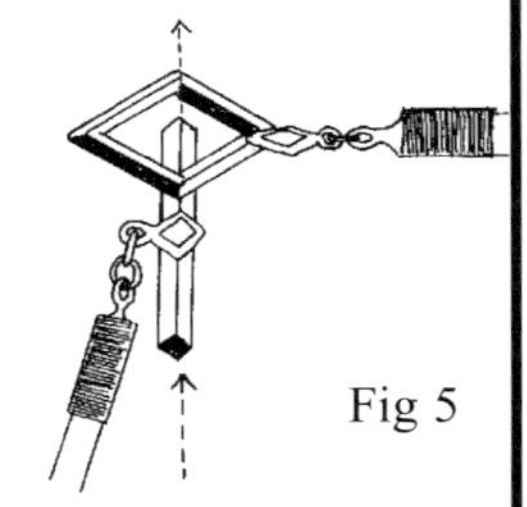

Fig 5

Fig 6

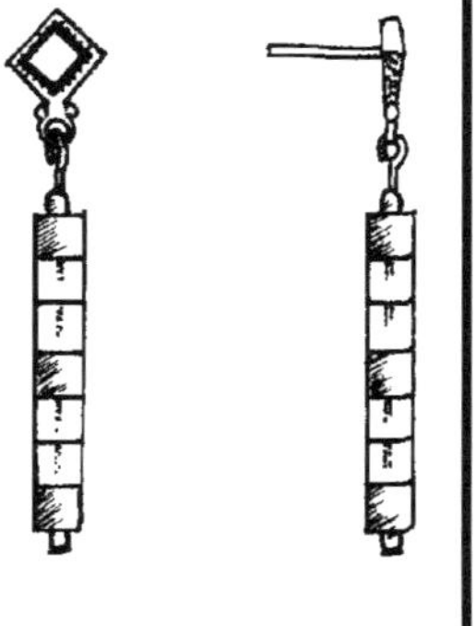

part of the toggle to be passed into its corresponding part.
**5.)** Repeat steps 2 & 3 on the other side.
**6.)** Connect the second part of the toggle to the crimp by one jump ring only (Fig.5).

## Matching Earrings

**Materials:**
2 x headpins
2 x 7mm diamond shaped stud
4 x silver size 8 seed beads
6 x 5mm metal cubed beads
8 x 5mm cubed crystals

**Tools:**
Round nose pliers
Cutters

**Method:**
**1.)** Thread beads on to both headpins as indicated in the picture or as desired.
2.) Follow the instructions for Standard Earrings -**project 2.**

## Project 6 - Cotton Thong Necklace

This is a valuable technique to master. You can lengthen or shorten this necklace easily depending on what neckline you are wearing. It is handy for making necklaces or bracelets to suit a variety of users. Simply adjust the length yourself by sliding the knot to and fro.
Make sure you have at least 30" of cotton for this project. You can always cut a bit off if needs be. Much less stringing will result in a necklace that won't go over your head!!

To make the necklace pictured you will need the following:

**Materials:**
30 " of 1.5mm cotton thong
1 x 20mm glazed ceramic bead
2 x 12mm glazed ceramic cushion
2 x 18mm glazed ceramic lozenge
2 x 8mm glazed ceramic round bead
2 x 4mm ceramic bead
10 x metal washers
Alternatively, substitute where desired

**Tools:**
Scissors

**Method:**
**1.)** Thread the beads onto the cotton thong in a sequence of your choice. Allow them to drop to the centre of the thonging.
**2.)** Working from the left hand, place your thumb 4" from the end of the thonging with your index finger underneath the thong.
**3.)** Using 8" of thong from the other end, * bend in half. Slip the thong at the bend underneath your left thumb (Fig. 1). Release the thong held with the right hand. You should have a configuration in the shape of an E with the thumb of the left hand keeping all three strands in place.
Now put your left leg through your arms followed by your right leg, then run around shouting that you've lost your marbles!! Rest assured, no one will doubt you.

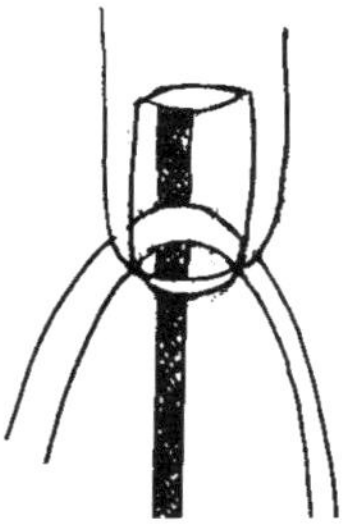
Fig 1

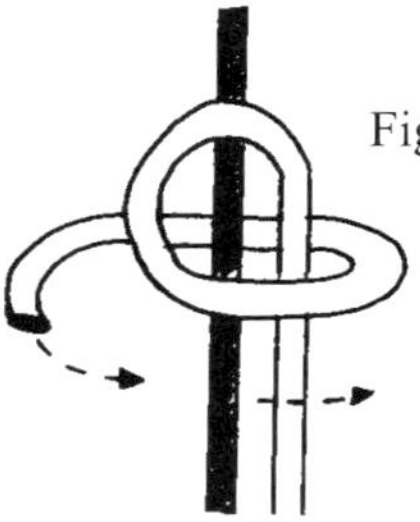
Fig 2

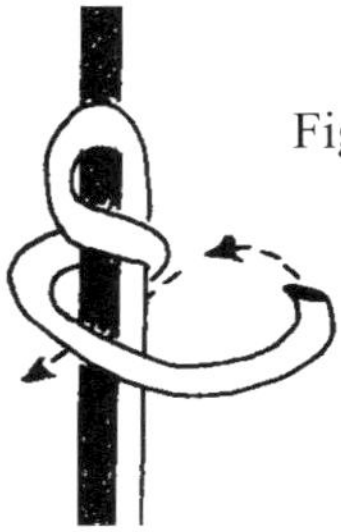
Fig 3

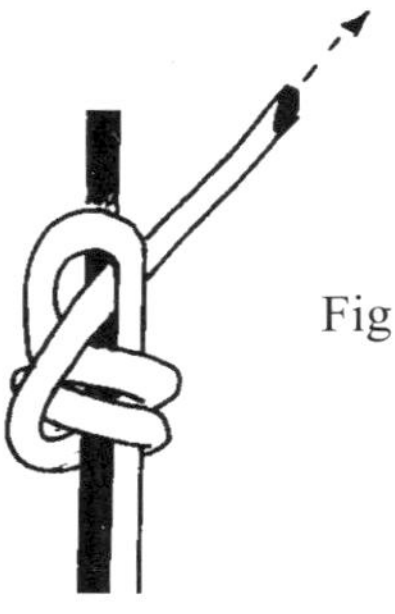
Fig 4

Fig 5

4.) With your right hand pick up the bottom line of the "E" and wrap it around the two above (Fig. 2). Wrap around once more (Fig.3).
**5.)** Slip the remaining 2" tail from the right hand through the loop held with the left (Fig. 4).
**6.)** Pull this knot together snugly (Fig. 5).
**7.)** With one knot complete and being held in your right hand, pull another 8" of thonging through this knot and proceed as from * of step 3.

Wear with pride - you've earned it !

## Matching Earrings

To make the earrings pictured you will need the following :

**Materials:**
2 x fish hooks
2 x head pins
6 x small plain cups
4 x metal washers
2 x 18mm ceramic lozenge
2 x 8mm ceramic round bead
Alternatively substitute where desired

**Tools:**
Round Nose Pliers
Cutters

**Method:**
Thread beads on to both headpins as indicated in the picture or as desired.
Follow the instructions for Standard Earrings - **project 2.**

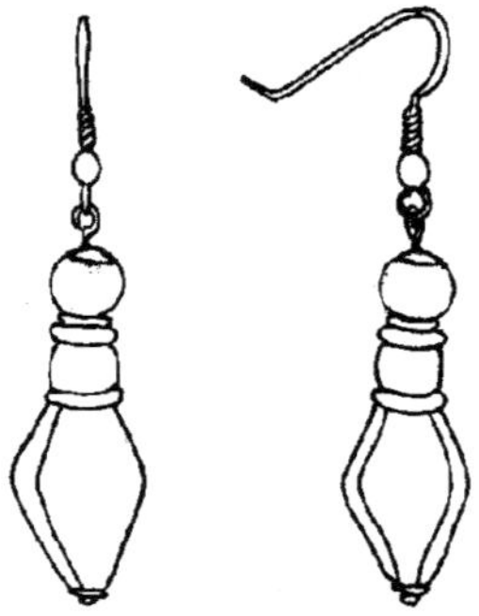

## Project 7 - Floating Necklace

This necklace is so called because the beads look like they are 'floating' on your neck because of the way the beads are spaced and kept in place. This style has been going for many years now and is still very popular. If you have never tried this technique before, it might be a good idea to read through the instructions and practice a little first on a small strand of tiger tail. You can always snip the beads off later and re-use them.

To make the necklace pictured you will need the following:

**Materials:**
Up to 50cm of 0.18 diameter, 7 strand, nylon coated wire (tiger tail)
2 x standard top opening calottes
2 x 4mm jump rings
1 x tag
1 x bolt ring
16 x crimps
7 x 8mm bicone beads
Alternatively, substitute where desired

**Tools:**
Round Nose Pliers
Chain Nose Pliers
Flush Cutters

**Method:**
**1.)** The findings quoted for this project take up 35mm.
Cut enough nylon coated wire to suit you, taking into account that the findings take up 35mm.
**2.)** Place a crimp over the end of the tiger tail as close to the edge as possible and pinch flat with the chain nose pliers. If there is any tiger tail protruding, cut it closely to the crimp.
**3.)** Slip a calotte on to the tiger tail so that it is ready to envelop the crimp (Fig. 2). Close the calotte as shown in Fig. 4 using a pliers or pinch it with your fingers. Slip a jump ring on to the hook of the calotte and pinch this hook closed. Open the jump ring again and add a tag. Close the

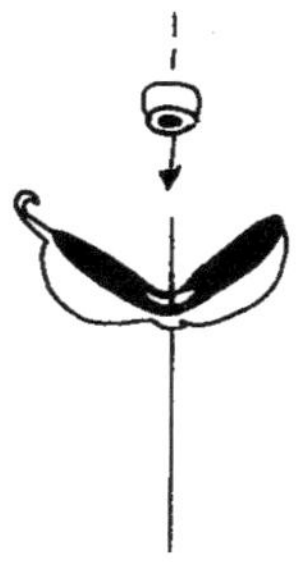

Fig 1

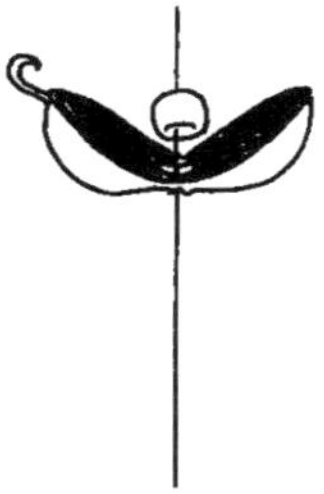

Fig 2

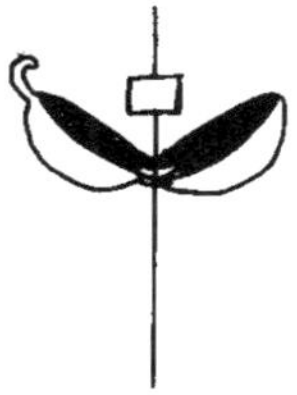

Fig 3

Fig 4

jump ring - see instructions in fig. 2 on page 18.

**4.)** Thread on a crimp, a bead, a crimp. Repeat this sequence 6 more times ending with a crimp.

**5.)** Carefully lay out the necklace on a design board leaving 2" gaps between each cluster of beads/crimps. Start by aligning the 4th bead with the 0 mark on the design board (Fig.6). Then position the other beads with 2" intervals either side of this one. Each bead should have a crimp at either side of it. If, for example you are making a 16" necklace make sure that both ends of the tiger tail do not go any further than the 7 1/2" mark on the design board. Allow one inch for fasteners. Check that all is in the correct position before proceeding any further.

**6.)** Place the index finger of your right hand on the tiger tail close to the calotte. This just stops the tiger tail from slipping while you proceed. Now carefully squash the crimps either side of each bead with the chain nose pliers (fig. 7). I usually start with the 4th bead then crimp the beads to the left and then the ones to the right. Do whatever is comfortable for you.

**7.)** Once all the beads are in place then add on the remaining calotte, remembering to slip it on in the other direction to the first one.

**8.)** Add a crimp, pinch it flat over the end of the tiger tail and close the calotte around it. Open the jump ring as per page 18 and slip the trigger catch on it. Close the jump ring.

Fig 5

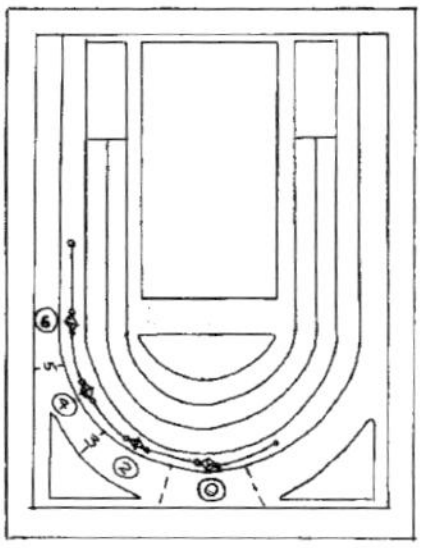

Fig 6

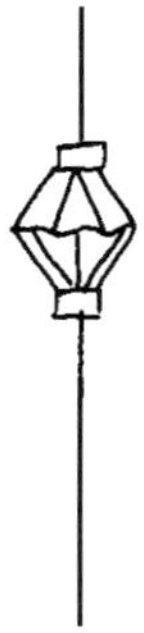

Fig 7

# Project 8 - Floating Earrings

Designed by Danielle Neilson

These are a delightful match to the floating necklace and demonstrate the usefulness of the side opening calotte. Alter the lengths and positions of tiger tail for variation.

To make the earrings pictured you will need the following:

**Materials:**
2 x fish hooks
2 x side opening calottes
2 x 8mm bicone bead
2 x 6mm bicone bead
2 x 4mm bicone bead.
2 x 25mm length tiger tail
2 x 38mm length tiger tail
2 x 50mm length tiger tail
8 x crimps
Alternatively, substitute where desired

**Tools:**
Chain Nose Pliers
Cutters

**Method:**
**1.)** Take the 50mm length of tiger tail and affix a crimp to the tip of it. Add the 8mm bicone bead on to the tiger tail. Repeat for the other 50mm strand. Set aside.
**2.)** Take the 38mm length of tiger tail and affix a crimp to the tip of it. Add the 6mm bicone bead on to the tiger tail. Repeat for the other 38mm strand. Set aside.
**3.)** Take the 25mm length of tiger tail and affix a crimp to the tip of it. Add a 4mm bicone bead on to the tiger tail. Repeat for the other 25mm strand. Set aside.
**4.)** Pick up one length of each size and ensure they are all even along the top. Position them together as you want them to be in the finished form. As pictured: from left to right, 6mm, 8mm then 4mm (Fig. 1). Place a crimp over all three strands and press the crimp together.

Fig 1

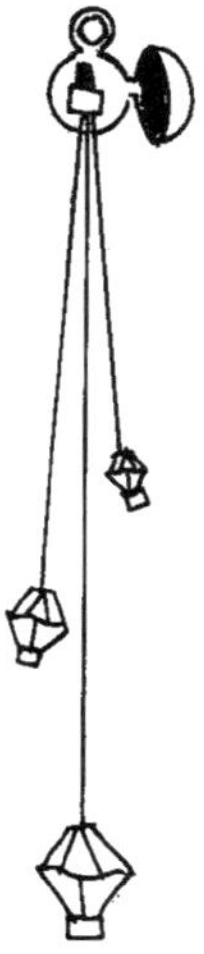

Fig 2

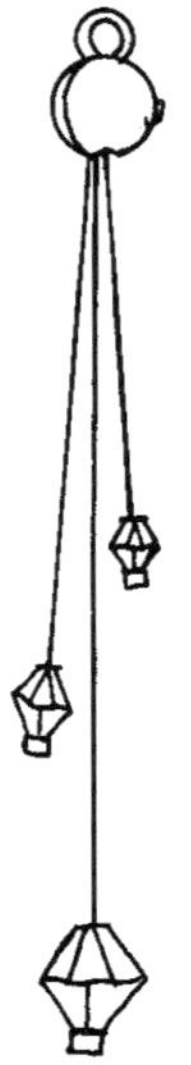

Fig 3

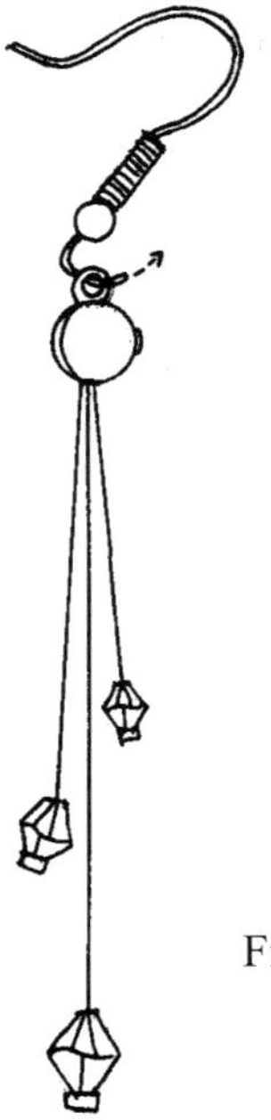

Fig 4

**5.)** Place the crimp with the attached beads into the open calotte (Fig. 2).
**6.)** Pinch the calotte closed (Fig 3).
**7.)** Open the loop of the fish hook and slip the calotte on to it (Fig 4).
**8.)** Repeat steps 1 to 4, remembering to reverse the sequence for the other earring as you want the pair of earrings to be a mirror image of each other.
**9.)** Repeat steps 5 to 7.

## Project 9 - Threaded Necklace

There are many ways to produce a threaded necklace. With the needle integrated into the thread the technique below is quick and hassle free. However, this material does fray and the needle is easily misshapen rendering it as a "use once only" product.

To make the necklace pictured you will need the following:

**Materials:**
1 x card of polyamid no. 6 thread with integrated needle
2 x top opening calottes
2 x 4mm jump rings
1 x tag
1 x trigger catch
11 x 10mm x 10mm square beads
22 x 6mm bicone beads to match square beads
50 x 4mm bicone beads to match above beads
Alternatively, substitute where desired

**Tools:**
Chain Nose Pliers
Scissors
Awl
Hypo Tube Cement

**Method:**
**1.)** Remove all thread from the card and straighten the needle.
**2.)** Make a knot on the opposite end to the needle (Fig. 1). Make another knot around this one.
**3.)** Thread on a calotte in the direction shown in Fig. 2, enveloping the knots.
**4.)** Cut off any excess thread and add glue allowing it to fully soak into the knots. Close the calottes (diags. 3 & 4).
**5.)** Add a jump ring on to the hook of the calotte. Pinch the hook closed. Open the jump ring as shown on page 18 and add a tag. Close the jump ring.
**6.)** Thread the beads on in the desired sequence.

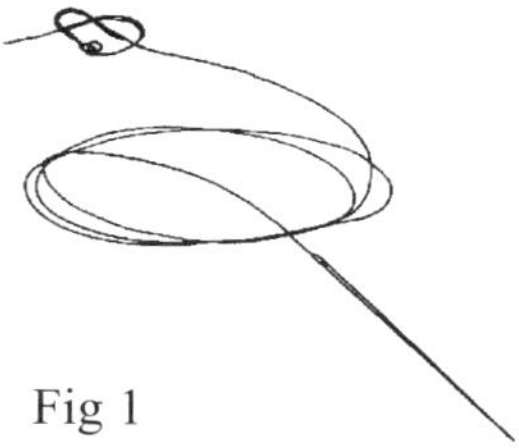
Fig 1

Fig 2

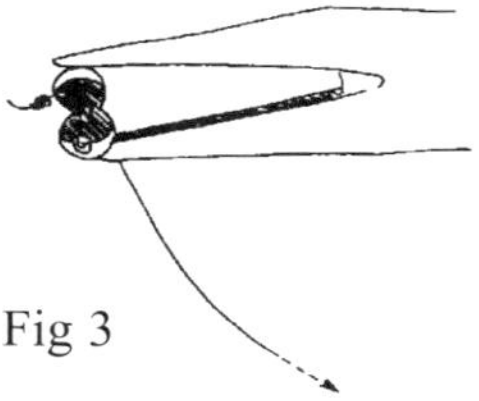
Fig 3

Fig 4

Fig 5

Fig 6

Fig 7

Fig 8

**7.)** When all the beads are in place, slip the remaining calotte on to the thread in the direction shown in Fig. 5, preparing to envelope the knot.

**8.)** As you are approaching the calotte/knotting from a different perspective you have to alter the way the knot is added in order to place the calotte/knot tight up against the last bead. If the thread is very tight against the calotte the necklace will have less fluidity. Leaving a large thread gap between the last bead and the calotte will expose the thread making it vulnerable. It also looks unsightly. Loosely make an overhand knot as before and slip the awl into the open part of the knot (Fig.6). With your right hand and using the awl, roll the knot towards the hole in the calotte while gently pulling the remaining thread with your left hand (Fig.7). Place the knot as closely as is necessary to the hole in the calotte. Make a second knot around this knot (Fig. 8). Add a tiny drop of glue. Close the calotte.

**9.)** Add a jump ring on to the hook of the calotte. Pinch the hook closed. Open the jump ring and add a catch. Close the jump ring.

Your necklace is ready to wear.

Fig A

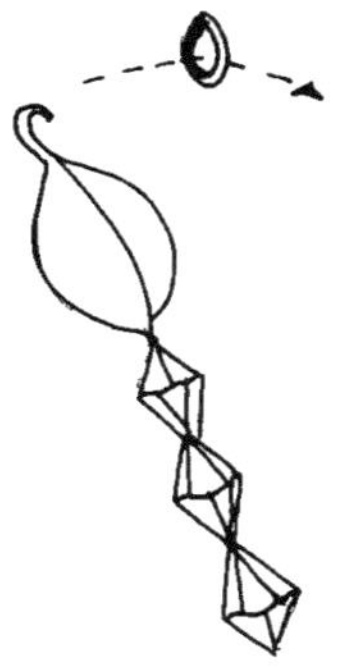

Fig B

Fig. C

Fig D

Fig E

Fig F

## Matching Earrings

To make the earrings pictured you will need the following

**Materials:**
2 x euro hooks
2 x head pins
4 x 2.5mm metal beads
4 x small fancy cups
2 x 10mm x10mm square beads
4 x 6mm bicone beads
4 x 4mm bicone beads
Alternatively substitute where desired

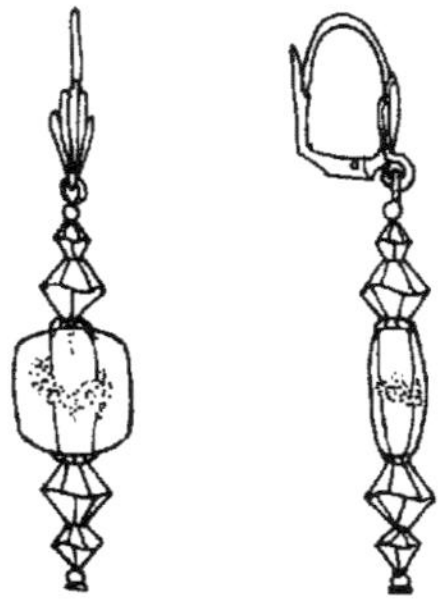

**Tools:**
Round Nose Pliers
Cutters

**Method:**
Thread the beads on to the head pin as depicted in the picture.
Follow instructions for Standard Earrings - **project 2**.

## Project 10 - Stud Earrings

The use of the claws in these earrings coupled with the facetted rhinestones gives the impression of a "setting". They look more expensive than they are and can be made 10 minutes before you leave the house. The claws are usually used to grip rhinestones onto fabric.
They can also be made by simply gluing the rhinestone directly on to the stud, though you must wait for the glue to dry. See the matching earrings for Project 12.

To make the earrings pictured you will need the following:

**Materials:**
2 x 7mm facetted glass rhinestones
2 x 8mm rhinestone claws
2 x scrolls
2 x 5mm flat pad studs
Alternatively, substitute where desired

**Tools:**
Bent Chain Nose Pliers

**Method:**
**1.)** Place the flat pad stud into the claw (Fig.1).
**2.)** Place the rhinestone on top of both of these (Figs. 2 & 3).
**3.)** Push all three components together with the index finger and thumb of your left hand. Grip both sides with the bent nose pliers with your right hand and gently pinch one 'point' of the claw over the rhinestone (Fig. 4). Getting this first one in position can be awkward. Once you get it in place it is easier to pinch the others. Pinch the 'point' at the opposite side next. Secure the remaining three points (Fig. 5).
**4.)** Repeat this procedure for the other earring.
**5.)** Push scrolls into place.

Your earrings are ready to wear.

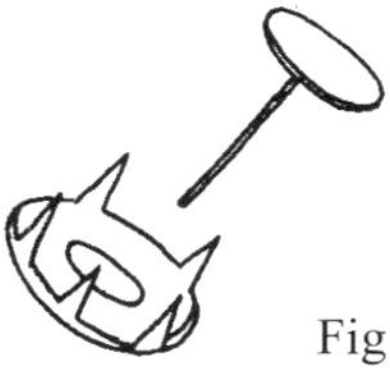
Fig 1

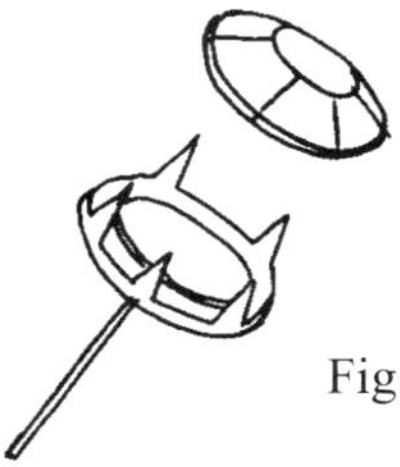
Fig 2

Fig 3

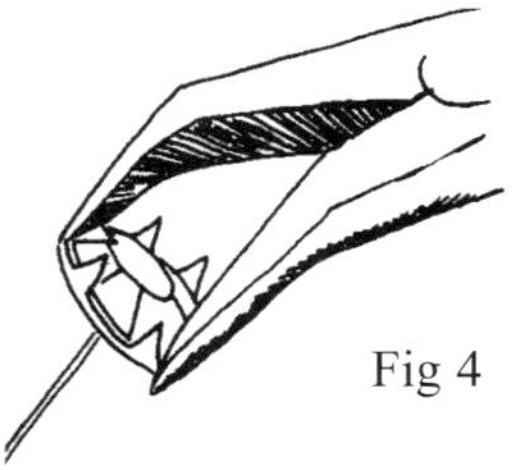
Fig 4

Fig 5

# Project 11 - Link Bracelet

Create a matching set of bracelet and necklace. Simply make more links for the necklace. It's that easy. The average bracelet length varies between 6" and 8".
If you find that the bracelet below doesn't fit your wrist properly using the links, try leaving out a link and add a few extra jump rings instead. It is important that bracelets fit correctly. When measuring your wrist measure over your knuckle bone.

To make the bracelet pictured you will need the following:

**Materials:** (to make a 7½ " bracelet)
10 x 6mm facetted beads
10 x eye pins
20 x 2.5mm metal beads
3 x 4mm oval jump rings
1 x toggle clasp
Alternatively, substitute where desired

**Tools:**
Round Nose Pliers
Chain Nose Pliers
Cutters

**Method:**
**1.)** Thread on a metal bead, a 6mm bead and a metal bead on to an eye pin (diags. 1 & 2). Make a loop as Standard Earrings - **project 2**.
**2.)** Make 10 of these links as per Fig. 3.
**3.)** Join them together by opening a loop and slipping this loop onto the loop of another link. Join all 10 links together (Fig. 4).
**4.)** Add a Toggle Clasp to the bracelet as per project 5, page 26.

Wear with pride. You've earned it.

Fig 1

Fig 2

Fig 3

Fig 4

## Project 12 - Necklace Without Findings

This technique allows you to finish a necklace using the same beads that are in the necklace. In this project I have used 1.0mm leather thong to match the diameter of the bead with the smallest hole. Use the thickest thonging possible.

To make the necklace pictured you will need the following:

**Materials:** (to make an 18" necklace)
16 x 12mm round handmade beads
16 x 8mm bicone beads
32 x 5mm beaded roundels
26" (66cm) of 1.0mm leather thong
2 x 5mm metal beads with a 3mm hole
8" of 0.4mm wire
Alternatively, substitute where desired

**Tools:**
Cutters

**Method:**
**1.)** Hold the leather at one end and fold the leather around to meet itself using the last 6cm of thong (Fig. 1).
**2.)** Take the wire and lash it around the last 5mm of folded thong (Fig. 2). If you are using beads sized differently to the ones pictured you must make this loop to slip over the intended bead firmly though not too tight. Check by holding the loop in place with your finger and thumb and slip this potential loop over the bead. When you are satisfied that the loop is adequate then lash/twist the wire around the two strands of thonging. Only add the amount of wire that will be hidden by the length of the metal bead with the large hole (Figs 3 & 4). Cut off excess wire to use at the other end.
**3.)** Slip one of the large holed metal beads over the loop just formed and let it rest on top of the wire work (Figs 3 & 4).
**4.)** Thread all the beads onto the leather thong as shown in the picture.
**5.)** With the last bead of the necklace in place, thread on the

Fig 1

Fig 2

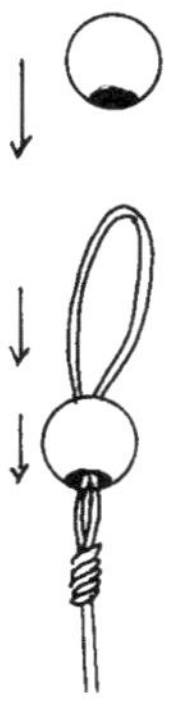
Fig 3

Fig 4

Fig 5

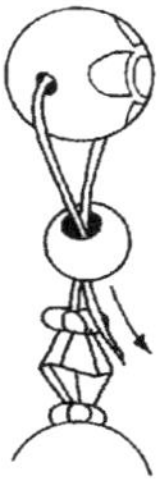

Fig 6

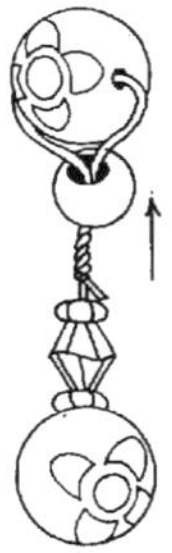

Fig 7

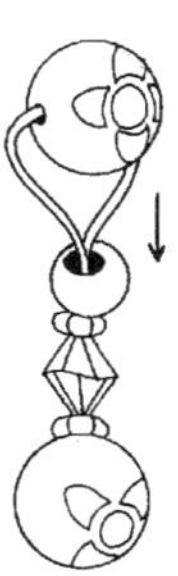

Fig 8

second metal bead and then the bead you want as a fastener (the 12mm handmade bead). Pass the leather through the metal bead again.

**6.)** Tug the thonging down so that you achieve the length you need (Fig. 5 and 6) which should be comfortably loose, approximately the same length as the loop at the beginning.

**7.)** Temporarily push the metal bead up towards the handmade bead, out of the way (Fig. 7).

**8.)** Lash the remaining wire around the two pieces of thonging as before. Trim off unwanted wire. Cut off the excess leather.

**9.)** Roll the metal bead back down over the wire work (Fig.8), hiding the wire.

## TIP

If you can't find a suitable metal bead with a large hole, leave it out. Make sure the wire work is neat.

Your necklace is ready to wear.
Wear with pride. You've earned it.

# Matching Earrings

These earrings are so easy, and inexpensive, to make. As you have the glue out make a few pairs in a variety of colours. To keep the studs in place and to prevent the glued rhinestones from sliding off the stud, spike the rod of the stud into a piece of sponge or cork before you start glueing.

To make a pair of stud earrings that match, you will need the following;

**Materials:**
2 x 7mm facetted glass rhinestones
2 x 5mm flat pad studs
I x tube E6000 glue
Alternatively, substitute where desired

**Tools:**
Bent Nose pliers
Piece of sponge, cork or foam

**Method:**
Insert the rod of the studs into the sponge. Add a tiny drop of glue onto each pad using a tooth pick or similar. Pick up the rhinestone with the pliers and drop it on top of the glued pad.
Look underneath the earring to check if the rhinestone is on straight while the glue is sticky.
Remember E6000 takes a long time to dry. Leave them until the next day before wearing otherwise you may be wearing them permanently!!

# Project 13 - Fairies and Angels

Fig 1

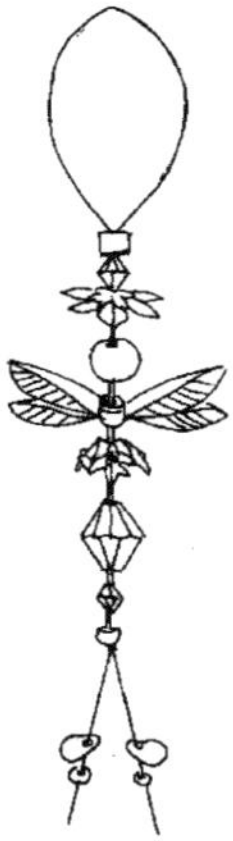

Fig 2

Fig 3

These can be hung in the window at any time of year or would make an unusual addition to your Christmas tree. The bicone beads I have used in this project are lead crystal which are brighter and more sparkly than glass beads. They give tiny little rainbows when light shines through them.

To make the fairy pictured you will need the following:

**Materials:**
24cm of 0.18 diameter, 7 strand tiger tail
4 x crimps
2 x 4mm lead crystal bicone beads
1 x 8mm lead crystal bicone bead
2 x 3mm side drilled drop beads
1 x flat 5 petal flower cup
1 x fairy wings
1 x coned floral cup
1 x 6mm round bead
Alternatively, substitute where desired

**Tools:**
Chain Nose Pliers
Cutters

**Method:**
**1.)** Bend the tiger tail in half. Slip a crimp up through both strands for at least 80mm, depending on how large you want the loop, and squash the crimp (Fig. 1).
**2.)** Thread all the beads on to both strands in the following sequence: 4mm bicone - flat flower cup - 6mm round bead - wings - coned cup - 8mm bicone - 4mm bicone - crimp.
**3.)** Slide all these beads towards the first crimp. Pinch the last crimp with the chain nose pliers, keeping the beads in place (Fig 2).
**4.)** Slip a drop bead and a crimp onto each strand. Pinch the crimps at the end of the tiger tail.
**5.)** You can make angels in the same way except substitute the flat flower cup with a scalloped rhinestone roundel (halo) and swap the fairy wings for angel wings. Remember to put the wings the right way up. Change the 6mm bicone bead (face) for a 6mm round pearl if you wish.

## Project 14 - Memory Wire Bracelet

As discussed in the Materials section this is an easy and durable wire. There are no findings to be attached. Don't be fooled, when it comes to bending this wire you really need to show it who's boss. When purchased in large quantities it looks much like a slinky.

To make the bracelet pictured you will need the following:

**Materials:**

1 & ½ coils large size bracelet memory wire
1 x 15mm diamond shaped cloisonné bead
2 x 8mm cloisonné beads
2 x 28mm cloisonné beads
18 x 2.5mm metal beads
22 - 24 x 4mm glass pearls
12 x seed beads
4 x small plain cups
Alternatively, substitute where desired

**Tools:**

Sturdy Cutters
Chain Nose Pliers
1 piece of sticky tack.

**Method:**

**1.)** Thread the beads onto the memory wire as shown in the picture as far as the long cloisonné beads remembering to put the cups either side of the 8mm round beads. These beads tend to wander up around the other side of the wire as you are working on your bracelet resulting in a lop-sided arrangement. To prevent this, add a small piece of sticky tack beside the last bead on the side you are not working on. This keeps the design in position (Fig. 1). Check that the feature beads (cloisonné beads featured along the top) are in the centre of the wire.

**2.)** With the beads centred and the sticky tack in place, add the seed beads and pearls. When the correct amount are in place and with about 10mm of memory wire left, grip the end of the wire with the chain nose pliers and roll the wire into a loop (Figs. 2 & 3), working against the curve of the

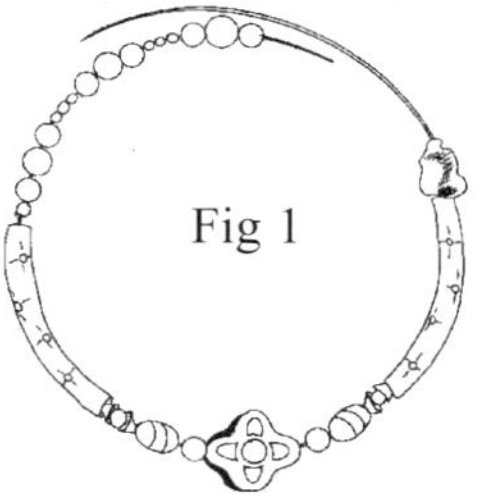

Fig 1

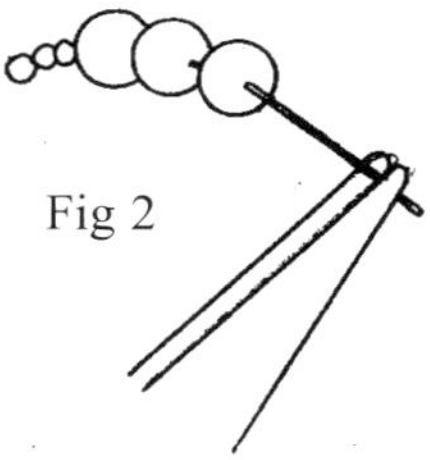

Fig 2

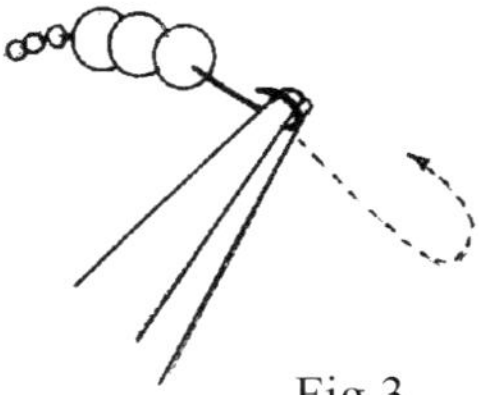

Fig 3

Fig 4

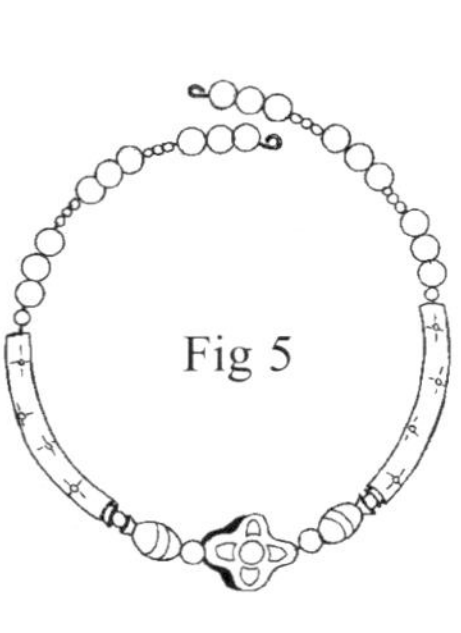

Fig 5

wire. It is important to note that if you roll the wire in the same direction as the curve, the loop you have formed will stick into your wrist and irritate you.
**3.)** Remove the sticky tack from the other side and work in the same way as step 2.

That's it. Your bracelet is ready to wear.

## Project 15 - Wine Identity Ring

Eight of these make a wonderful house warming gift or just pop one into your purse to identify your own glass when at a party.

To make the wine I.D. ring pictured you will need the following ;

**Materials:**
8 x 4mm bicone beads
2 x 6mm bicone beads
4 x small fancy cups
1 x oval jump ring
1 x  charm of your choice
2 x tiny beaded rondels
2 x 2.5mm metal beads
1 and ¼ coils ring size memory wire
Alternatively, substitute where desired

**Tools:**
Sturdy Cutters
Chain Nose Pliers

**Method:**
**1.)** Add the jump ring onto the charm.
**2.)** Make a loop in the memory wire as described in project 14. Thread half the beads on as shown in picture.
**3.)** Slip the jump ring with the charm attached on to the memory wire. Thread on the rest of the beads.
**4.)** With all the beads threaded on, make a loop as before.

Your Wine I.D is ready for use, simply slip it on to the stem of a wine glass. Cheers!

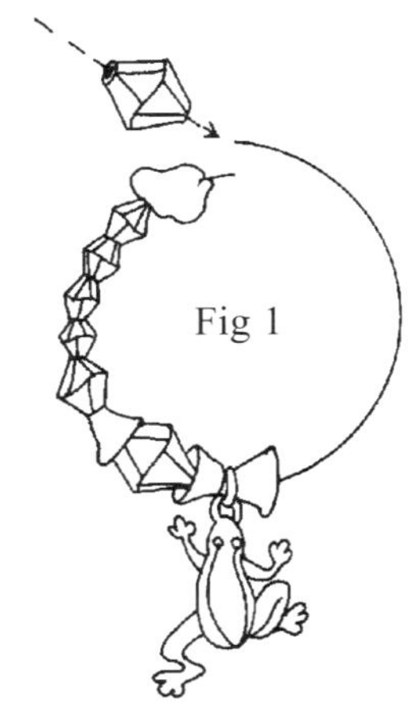


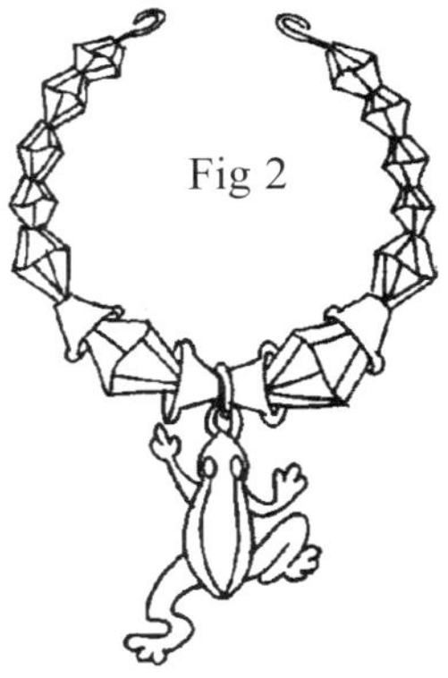

Fig 1

Fig 2

Fig 3

Combining the two techniques learned between standard earrings and the memory wire bracelet result in this delicate choker.

To make the choker pictured you will need the following:

**Materials:**
1 & ½ coils of choker memory wire
44 x 2.5mm metal beads
24 x 3mm metal bugle beads
17 x 4mm bicone beads
9 x 6mm bicone beads
3 x 8mm bicone beads
9 x headpins
Alternatively, substitute where desired

**Tools:**
Cutters
Sturdy Cutters
Round Nose Pliers
Chain Nose Pliers

**Method:**
This choker is made up in three stages.
Stage 1 is the construction of nine 'drops'
Stage 2 is positioning these 'drops' in the front of the choker.
Stage 3 is adding the finishing beads to the rest of the choker.

**Stage 1**
Using the Standard Earring technique on page 21, make three 'drops' of different lengths:
Three long (Fig. 1)
Two medium (Fig. 2)
Four short (Fig.3)

**Stage 2**

Thread the beads and drops onto the memory wire carefully following the sequence as shown in Fig.4, taking note of the positioning of the different length 'drops'.

When they are all in place, roll this series of beads along so that they are sitting in the centre of the memory wire with an equal amount of bare memory wire either side.

**Stage 3**

Add a piece of sticky tack beside the last bead at one side to keep this run of beads in place.

Thread the bugle beads onto the side without the sticky tack.

Make a loop as described in project 14 (Memory Wire Bracelet).

Remove the sticky tack and add the bugle beads to this side. Make a loop as before.

Your choker is ready to wear.

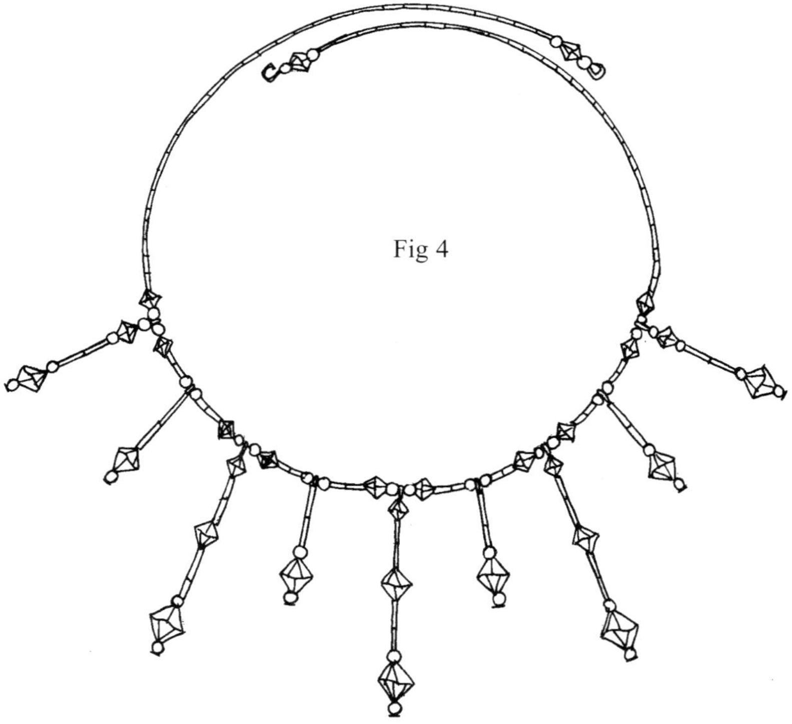

Fig 4

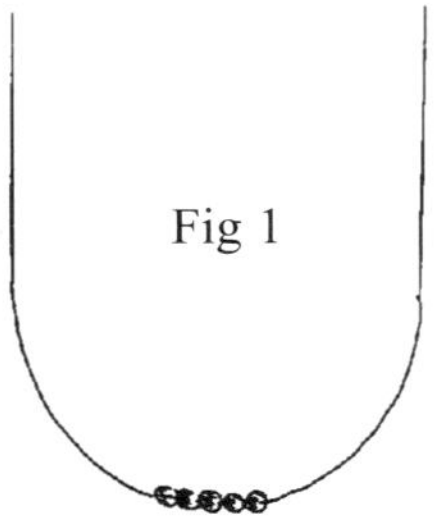

Fig 1

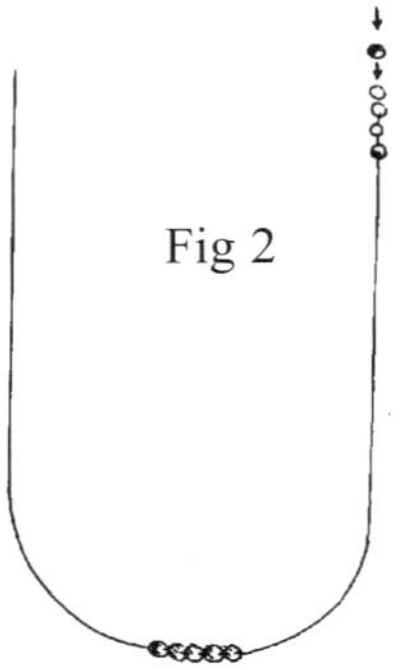

Fig 2

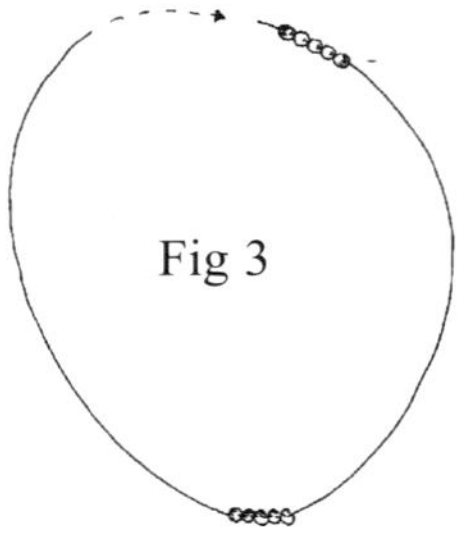

Fig 3

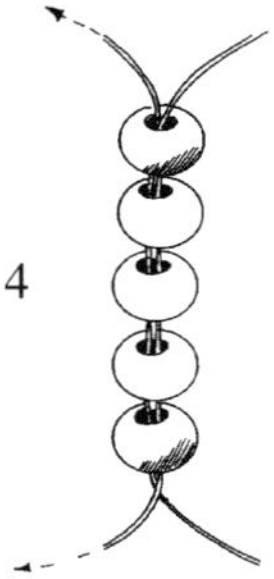

Fig 4

At first glance this necklace looks too complex to include in a 'Basic' Jewellery Making book. But when this project is broken down into step by step segments it is surprisingly easy, once you have got the gist of this technique. Try experimenting with different shapes - triangles, diamonds, rectangles or hexagons.

To make the necklace pictured you will need the following:

**Materials:** (to make a 17 ½ " necklace)
1 packet of size 8 seed beads - main colour, referred to as M
1 packet of size 8 seed beads to complement the first colour, referred to as C
16 x 4mm facetted beads
25cm (approx. 10") of 3mm belcher chain
1 x spool of 28 gauge wire
11 x eye pins
2 x oval jump rings
1 catch
Alternatively, substitute where desired

**Tools:**
Round Nose Pliers
Chain Nose Pliers
Bent Nose Pliers

**Method:**
This necklace has three phases.
Phase 1 is making the 5 wired pendants.
Phase 2 is making the 6 links.
Phase 3 is assembling the above components with the chain.
You can alter the length of this necklace by adding or subtracting beaded links or chain.

**Phase 1: Pendants**
**1.)** Cut a length of the wire 36cm ( approx. 14" ) long.
**2.)** Thread on 5 main beads and allow them to drop to the

centre of the wire (Fig. 1).

**3.)** Pick up 1 main, 3 contrast and 1 main bead on the right hand piece of wire (Fig. 2).

**4.)** Pass the wire of the left hand through the beads on the right (Fig.3).

**5.)** Pull both wires (diags 4 & 5) until the second set of beads sits on top of the first set (Fig. 6).

**6.)** Continue in this way for 5 rows, following the pattern shown (Fig. 7). Main beads are shown shaded and contrast beads are plain white.

**7.)** Cut off excess wire leaving a 6cm tail at both sides.

**8.)** Wrap this wire around the wire on the outside edge (Fig. 8). Wind wire down for two rows. Cut off surplus wire and flatten any protruding wire.

**9.)** Thread 2 main beads, a 4mm bead and 2 main beads on to an eye pin (Fig. 9).

**10)** Pick up the square of beads just completed and turn it upside down so that you have the first row pointing north. The reason for this is because the first row only has one strand of wire going through it, making it easier to insert the eye pin.

**11)** With the 5 beads threaded on to the eye pin in step 9, pass this eye pin through the first row of beads as discussed above (Fig. 10).

**12)** Put 2 main beads, a 4mm bead and 2 main beads on to this eye pin (Fig. 11). Form a loop at the end of this eye pin.

**13)** Make four more of these pendants.

**Phase 2: Links**

**1.)** Make 4 beaded links as described in the link bracelet project on page 38 using 2 main, a 4mm bead and 2 main.

**2.)** Make 2 beaded links using 1 main, a 4mm bead and 1 main.

**3.)** Cut the chain into 10 segments of 6 complete links.

**Phase 3: Assembly**

**1.)** Open the eye of one of the pendants and slip the first link of a piece of chain on to it. Close the eye.

**2.)** Open the eye of a 5 beaded link and slip the sixth link of the chain on to it.

Fig 5

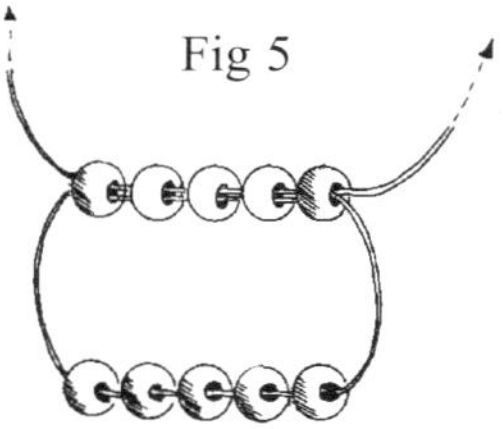

Fig 6

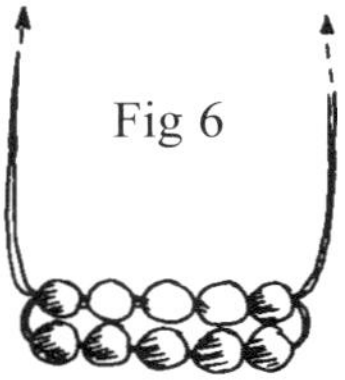

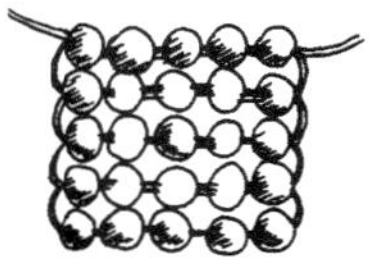

Fig 7

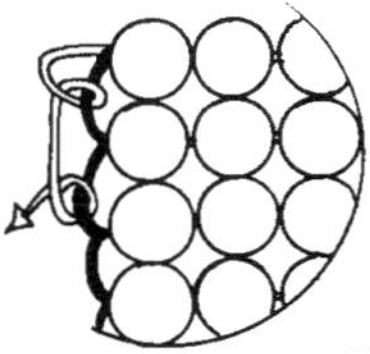

Fig 8

Fig 9

**3.)** Open the eye at the other end of the beaded link and slip another piece of chain onto this eye. Close this eye.
**4.)** Open the eye of a pendant and slip the sixth link of chain on to this pendant.
**5.)** Continue in this way, opening eye pins and connecting each phase by chain (Fig. 12). When you reach the last piece of chain, add on the 3 beaded links to both sides.
**6.)** Open the eye pin of this last beaded link and attach the catch via a jump ring.
**7.)** Attach the corresponding part to the other side.

Wear with pride. You've earned it.

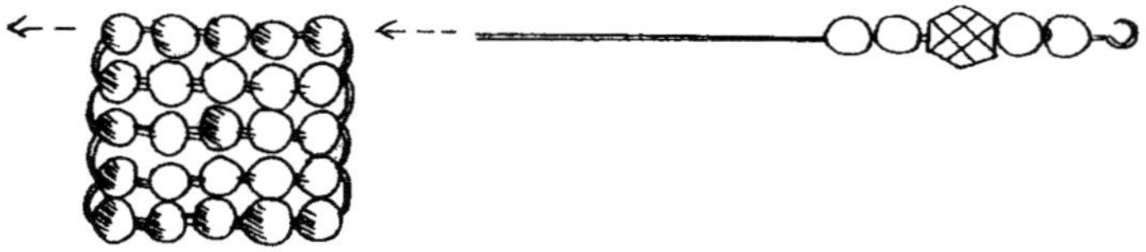

Fig 10

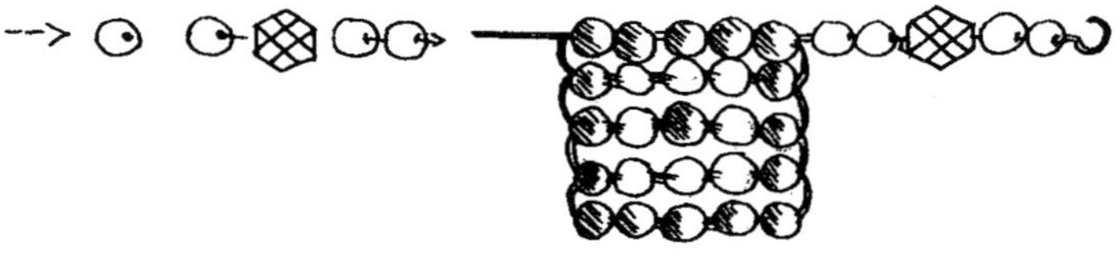

Fig 11

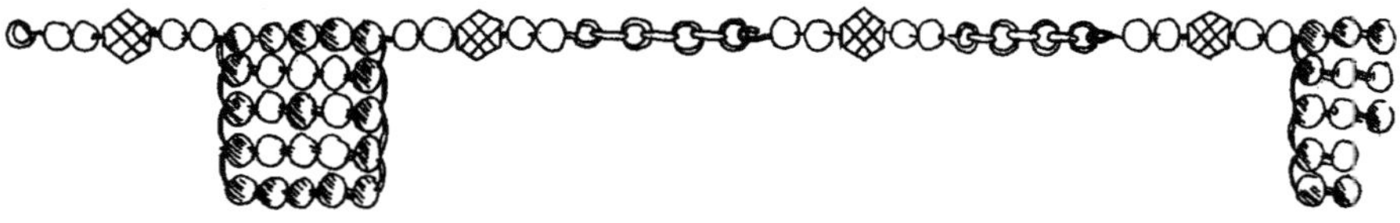

Fig 12

## Matching Earrings

Make earrings to match the necklace by following steps 1 to 8 in phase 1 with the exceptions listed below.

To make the earrings pictured you will need the following ;
Alternatively substitute where desired.

**Materials:** (to make 1 pair of earrings)
30 size 8 seed beads in main colour
16 size 8 seed beads in a complementary colour to the main colour
2 x 36cm lengths of 28 gauge wire
2 x fish hooks
2 x horizontally drilled drop beads
Alternatively, substitute where desired

**Tools:**
Chain Nose Pliers
Bent Nose pliers
Cutters

**Method:**
Instead of adding 5 main beads on the first row, add 2 main, a horizontally drilled drop and 2 main beads.
Continue with pattern until the last row where you only add 4 main beads instead of 5.
Open the eye of the fish hook and slip eye into the gap left between the second and third beads on the last row.

# Project 18 - Organza Necklace

Fig 3

Fig 4

Fig 5

Fig 6

This is a soft, feminine necklace. The beads used (gemstone chips ) have a relatively small hole so they need to be pulled along the organza with great care to avoid laddering this material. Other beads do not add this complication. It is surprising how the beads just sit where you want them to. If your favourite bead glides on a little too easily, simply tie a knot in the organza either side of the bead to keep it in place.

To make the necklace pictured you will need the following;

**Materials:** (to make an 18" necklace)
20 - 26 approx. x amethyst gemstone chips
12 - 16 approx. x 3mm metal beads
1 and ½ meters of 8mm organza ribbon
2 x large side opening calottes
2 x 4mm jump rings
1 x bow catch
1 x butterfly pendant
Alternatively, substitute where desired

**Tools:**
1 x big eye needle
Hypo Tube Cement
Bent nose pliers or chain nose pliers

**Method:**
**1)** Fold the organza in half and slip the needle on to it. Bring the big eye needle to the centre of this fold. There appears to be a disproportionate amount of organza compared to the finished length. You will be making two knots at either end of your necklace. There is nothing worse than trying to form a knot with an inadequate amount of threading material.
**2)** Pass the needle and organza through both loops at the back of the butterfly pendant (Fig 1, opposite page). Ensure that there are equal lengths of organza exiting both sides of the butterfly.
**3)** Remove the needle by cutting the organza (Fig. 2).

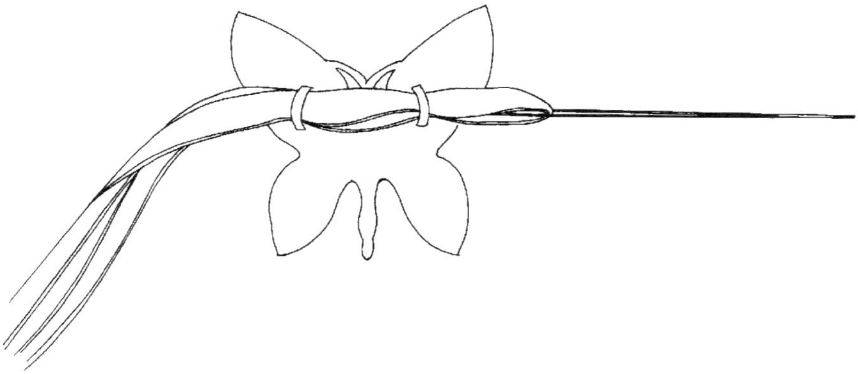

Fig 1

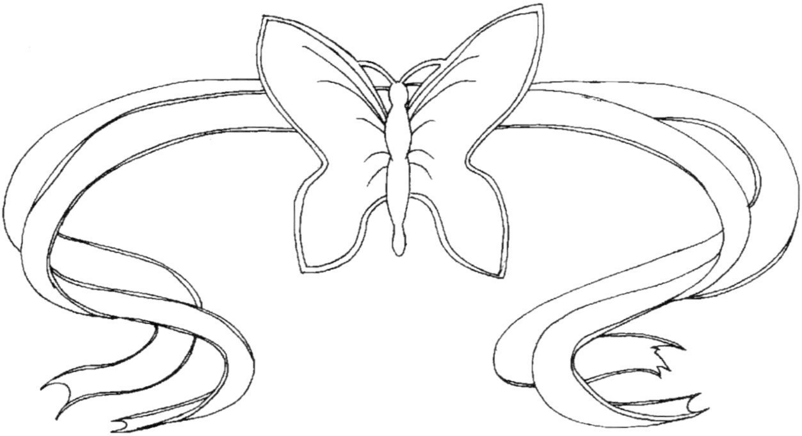

Fig 2

Fig 7

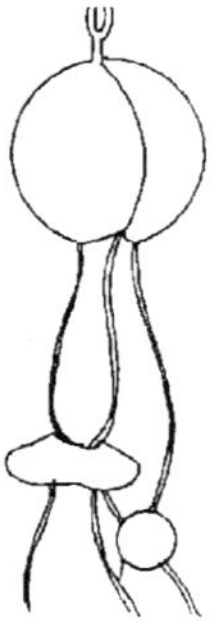

Fig 8

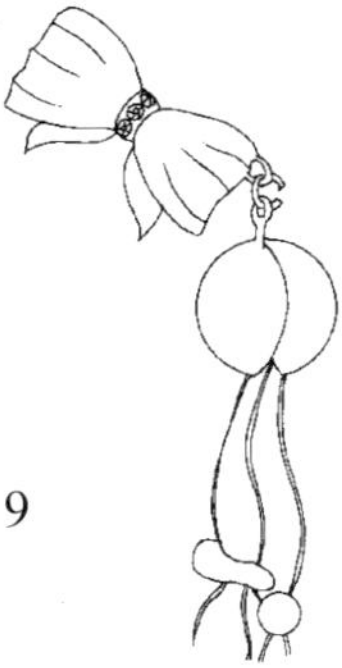

Fig 9

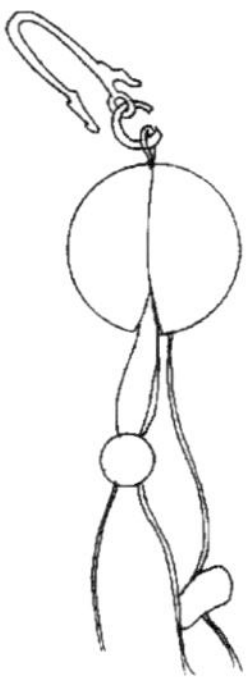

Fig 10

**4)** Randomly thread the chips and metal beads onto each ribbon individually using the following technique:
The ribbon has a rib running down both sides of it. Cut precisely along the edge of this rib for between 15mm to 20mm then gradually slope the cut to the opposite side (Fig. 3). You have formed a 'needle'. Slide a bead onto the "needle" and carefully draw it down along the ribbon (Fig.4). Continue to add beads and chips randomly on to all four strands.
Refrain from adding beads right up to the end of the ribbon as you will need some free material to manoeuvre knots for closure into place, a gap of about 2" (10 mm ) is ample.
**5)** Once you are satisfied that all beads are *in situ* turn the pendant over so that you have the reverse side facing you. Measure the distance from the centre of the pendant to end of the organza. Both sides should be of equal length.
Pick up the double strands of organza on the left hand side and roll them together into a loose knot 8 ½ inches from the centre of the pendant (Fig. 5). Repeat for the right hand strands.
When you are completely satisfied that all beads are in the correct position and the strands are the required lengths, tighten all knots (Fig. 6).
**6)** Cut off any excess ribbon and add the glue, allowing the Hypo Tube Cement to be fully absorbed into the knots. Clamp the calotte closed around the knot with the pliers (Figs. 7 and 8). Repeat for the other side.
**7)** Open the jump ring as shown on page 18. Put the loop of the calotte on to the open jump ring and slip the loop of the catch on to the open jump ring also (Fig. 9). Close the jump ring.
**7a )** Open another jump ring and add the loop of the calotte on to this jump ring at the other side. Slip the corresponding part of the catch on to the jump ring also. Close the jump ring.

Your necklace is ready to wear.

# Notes